THE TOTAL BLUES KEYBOARDIST

>> A Fun and Comprehensive Overview of Blues Keyboard Playing

DAVID GLEASON

Alfred, the leader in educational music publishing,

and the National Guitar Workshop,

one of America's finest guitar schools, have joined

forces to bring you the best, most progressive

educational tools possible. We hope you will enjoy

this book and encourage you to look for

other fine products from Alfred and the

National Guitar Workshop.

Alfred Music Publishing Co., Inc.
P.O. Box 10003
Van Nuys, CA 91410-0003
alfred.com

ISBN-10: 0-7390-7524-1 (Book & CD)
ISBN-13: 978-0-7390-7524-1 (Book & CD)

This book was acquired, edited, and produced
by Workshop Arts, Inc., the publishing arm of
the National Guitar Workshop.
Nathaniel Gunod, acquisitions, managing editor
Burgess Speed, acquisitions, senior editor
Timothy Phelps, interior design
Ante Gelo, music typesetter
CD recorded and mastered by Collin Tilton at Bar None Studio, Northford, CT
David Gleason (keyboards), Burgess Speed (guitar and drums)

Cover photographs:
Electronic keyboard courtesy Korg USA, Inc.
Inset photo © Niki Rossi Photography
www.nikirossi.com

 Alfred Cares. Contents printed on 100% recycled paper.

Contents

About the Author

David Gleason is a keyboardist, bandleader, and music educator who teaches music theory, music history, jazz ensembles, and drumming at the John Sayles School of Fine Arts in Schenectady, NY. He has also taught ethnomusicology at the Rensselaer Polytechnic Institute.

Gleason received an M.A. in music from Tufts University where he studied ethnomusicology and composition. As an ethnomusicologist, he researched Caribbean folk and popular music in Puerto Rico and Cuba. He also holds a B.M. in music education, with a jazz studies minor, from the Crane School of Music (SUNY Potsdam).

As a pianist, he has performed with John Fedchock, Danilo Perez, Laurel Massé of The Manhattan Transfer, Fred Wesley, The Either/Orchestra, The Boston Latin Band, Rumbanama, Soul Session, The Big Soul Ensemble, and The Joey Thomas Big Band. He currently leads the acclaimed Latin jazz ensemble Sensemaya, which recently released their first album, *Shake It!*

Gleason has recorded keyboard tracks for several Alfred/NGW books, including *Drum Atlas: Brazil*, *Drum Atlas: Cuba, Drum Atlas: Salsa,* and *The Total Funk Drummer.*

PHOTO BY BILL ZISKIN

For more information about the author and his music, please visit: www.sensemaya.net

Acknowledgements

Thanks to all of the excellent piano teachers I have studied with over the years, especially Rose Reed, Suzanne Lavigne, Lee Shaw, and Dr. Gary Busch. This book goes out to them and all of the other piano teachers in the world. It's because of their efforts and patience that great piano music lives on. Thanks to my family, especially my wife, Mary; my daughter, Maryn; and my hound dog, Kingston. Without their support this book would not have been possible. Thanks also to Pete Sweeney for getting me involved with the National Guitar Workshop and to Burgess Speed for his support and flexibility. Thanks to Lisa and Marc Schonbrun for their computer help. Thanks to my brother, Matt, for accompanying me on a blues pilgrimage. Thanks also to my parents and my Uncle Johnny, for playing all of those 45s of great blues, rhythm and blues, and rock and roll for me when I was a kid. Special thanks to my father and my uncle for taking me to play at my first blues jam session—this book is a direct result of that day.

Introduction

The blues is at the heart of American music. When you learn to play the blues, you are delving into a tradition that spans more than a century. This tradition underlies the performance of blues music; it expresses the struggles, joys, and everyday life of generations of Americans. Since so many styles of music are derived from or influenced by the blues, learning to play it is a bit like a homeward journey into the center of American music. For a keyboard player, this book provides the road map.

The Total Blues Keyboardist is useful to keyboard students at all levels. It provides a detailed study of blues styles, blues-oriented music theory, and blues keyboard technique. The book is divided into three parts. Part 1 provides essential information about musicianship, basic keyboard technique, music reading, and music theory. It can be used as a comprehensive review, or as a source for learning these skills for the first time. Part 2 explores the many regional and individual styles associated with the blues. Since the blues is central to so many types of music, its influence on jazz, gospel, and funk are also addressed. This is particularly important because these styles have in turn influenced later generations of blues musicians. In each chapter, culture, history, and style elements are presented along with technical information and pieces to practice and perform. As the book progresses through the history of the blues, the difficulty of the pieces increases. With each musical example, a recording is provided for you to listen to and play along with. Part 2 also introduces elements of improvisation. Part 3 presents information about playing with other musicians, advanced improvisation, composition, and challenging keyboard techniques. As you progress through this book, you are encouraged to revisit earlier chapters frequently; doing so will broaden your understanding of the songs, styles, and music theory you have already learned.

While this book provides a complete curriculum for learning to play blues keyboard, there are several ways to supplement it. As you learn to play the blues, you should immerse yourself in the great blues recordings. A list of suggested recordings is provided for you to begin your collection (see pages 126–127). When possible, go to performances and enjoy hearing live blues. Listening to real music always provides context to the type of information any book provides. It is also encouraged to find opportunities to express your creativity through playing with others and performing your own music. This will help you apply the concepts learned in this book in a truly artistic setting. Most of all, as you proceed through this book, be sure to tackle each page with grounded focus. Practice and perform with a clear relaxed mind. Finding your personal musical space will allow you to absorb the ideas more readily and lead to greater success.

Enjoy your blues journey!

A compact disc is available with this book. Using the disc will help make learning more enjoyable and the information more meaningful. Listening to the CD will help you correctly interpret the rhythms and feel of each example. The symbol to the left appears next to each song or example that is performed on the CD. Example numbers are above the symbol. The track number below each symbol corresponds directly to the song or example you want to hear.

PART 1: THE BASICS
Chapter 1: Getting Started

Typical Blues Keyboard Instruments

Keyboard instruments have been an exciting way to make music for centuries. The basic design consists of a series of black and white keys laid out in front of the performer. These keys can be easily pressed down to make a sound. In different types of keyboard instruments, different mechanisms are used to make sound. While you can have many variations of keyboard instruments and sounds, the physical layout of the keys is always the same.

Pianos

The piano is the most traditional of the blues keyboard instruments. Inside a piano, the keys control felt-covered hammers that strike strings. Pianos have been around since the 1700s. A few varieties of pianos are likely to be used for blues playing; the old honky-tonks and bars across the South often had upright pianos while the concert halls and recording studios had larger, more sonorous grand pianos (see photos below).

Upright piano.

Grand piano.

Organs

The organ is the original keyboard instrument. In the early church organs, air was used to vibrate large pipes. Blues musicians often use the electric organ. While a number of types exist, the most famous is the Hammond B-3. It has a rich and powerful tone, especially when played through Leslie speakers. Leslie speakers rotate the air and sound to create a wavering effect. Organs provide the performer with other ways to alter the sound as well. Sliding *drawbars,* manipulated like the faders on an audio mixing board, allow the performer to separate out different qualities of the tone. In this way, organists can get a variety of different sounds from the instrument. Many organs also come with effects for tone, percussion, and vibrato.

PHOTO BY CLIFF, ARLINGTON, VA

Hammond B-3 organ.

Electric Pianos

Blues musicians—especially those interested in soul, funk, and rhythm and blues—often choose to play electric pianos rather than acoustic ones. Electric pianos work similarly to an electric guitar and produce a uniquely modern tone. Depending on the model, sound is generated by an internal hammer that strikes a string, metal reed, or rod. This sound is then amplified electronically. Electric pianos were the first keyboard instruments to be portable, which made them popular among touring musicians. Starting in the 1960s, blues musicians played one of two major varieties of electric piano: the Fender Rhodes or the Wurlitzer electric piano. Musicians tend to refer to them by their nicknames, "Rhodes" and "Wurlie."

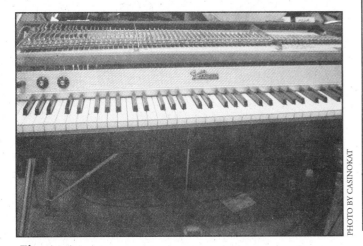

PHOTO BY CASINOKAT

Electric piano.

Electronic Keyboards

Unlike electric pianos, electronic keyboards produce their sound completely from electronic sound synthesizers. In other words, they don't have any hammers or strings inside. They started being used by blues musicians in the 1970s and have become very popular as computer technology allowed them to be light, portable, and produce better sounds. Nowadays, many blues musicians bring one or more electronic keyboards to a gig and use them to emulate the classic sounds of a B-3 organ, piano, or electric piano.

PHOTO COURTESY OF YAMAHA

Electronic keyboard.

Keyboard Posture

Playing a keyboard instrument requires good posture and technique. Correct playing will help you avoid strain on your muscles and joints. There are two basic postures for playing keyboard instruments: sitting and standing.

Sitting at the Keyboard

A seated posture is the most common way to play a keyboard instrument. To achieve a correct sitting position, start by adjusting the bench or chair to a height that allows the elbow to rest freely from the shoulder. At this height, your forearm should be parallel to the floor. For shorter keyboardists, it may be necessary to add cushions to the bench to reach the right height. Place the bench at a distance from the instrument that allows both forearms to be in a natural position at your sides. Sit on the front middle edge of the bench with your back in a naturally straight position. The idea is to sit up straight, but in a relaxed manner. You don't want to slouch, but you also don't want to be so rigid that you are adding stress to your wrists, arms, or back. Once you are seated comfortably and correctly at the instrument, you can be sure to get the best sound from it.

Standing at the Keyboard

Standing while playing a keyboard instrument is a relatively new development. In rock, Latin, and (sometimes) blues bands, it is appropriate to stand at an electronic keyboard rather than sit. This can add energy to the performance and create great visuals for the audience. In order to achieve a good standing posture, be sure to set the height of the keyboard stand so that your forearms are parallel to the floor while resting naturally from the shoulder. If the keyboard is positioned too high, you will put pressure on your wrists. If the keyboard is too low, you will likely put stress on your upper back. Make sure you are standing up straight, yet comfortably. If one foot is resting on a damper or volume pedal, it helps to position the other foot back slightly to achieve a balanced stance.

Correct sitting position.

Correct standing position.

Hand Position

Keyboard instruments are played with the hands. That makes hand position on the instrument very important. To establish the correct hand position, follow these guidelines:

1. Once you are seated or standing at the instrument, place your hands on the keys.

2. Round your fingers slightly so that the joints are all bent inward. Playing with the joints straight or bent back will not give you much power or flexibility. You can practice this position by holding a tennis ball in the palm of your hand, then trying to achieve a similar position on the keys.

While the fingers play with the tips, the thumb plays the keys on the side of its tip. This should feel natural and give the thumb the ability to "anchor" the hand with its weight. Look at your wrists. Be sure they are not flexed below the fingers or elevated high above them. The wrists should be raised very slightly above the point at which they are parallel to the forearm. This will provide strength at the instrument without causing stress to your arms or wrists. No matter what kind of keyboard instrument you are playing, when the keys are pressed, be sure that the fingers remain arched and do not flex their joints backwards or straighten out. At instruments with weighted keys, such as the piano, a good sound can be achieved using good wrist motion and arm weight in addition to finger strength.

Correct hand position.

Healthy Playing

If you follow the guidelines above, you are on your way to developing healthy keyboard technique. You must also listen to your body and avoid any motions that cause pain. Be sure to avoid any movements that are "clenched" or "tight." Tension is the enemy of healthy playing. Try to make your playing relaxed and fluid. Also, avoid practicing for endless hours. Take practice breaks; don't try to be a "keyboard superhero." If you feel unusual pain, see a doctor.

Organization of the Keyboard

The keys on pianos, organs, electric pianos, and electronic keyboards all have the same layout. Long white keys alternate with short black ones positioned in a repeating order. Pianos have 88 keys, while other keyboard instruments may have fewer. The black keys appear in groups of two or three, with each group separated by two consecutive white keys. All other black keys are separated by one white key. See below.

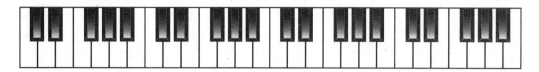

Each key on the keyboard is called by a note name that represents a musical pitch, or tone. Musicians use the *musical alphabet,* the letters A through G, to name notes. Look for any group of three black keys. Find the black key on the right end of this group. The white key just to the left of this black key is always called "A." From there, you can label all of the white keys alphabetically as you move to the right. After reaching "G," you begin again with "A." Moving from left to right on the keyboard, you will notice the pitch rises with each subsequent note. For this reason, we refer to the left end of the keyboard as "low" and the right end as "high." If you move from right to left, you are going "down" the keyboard; if you go in the opposite direction, you are moving "up" the instrument.

Low   High

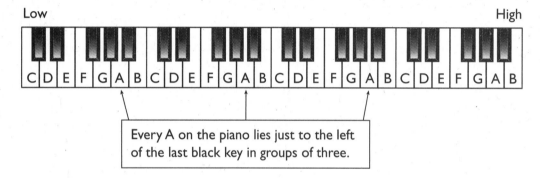

Every A on the piano lies just to the left of the last black key in groups of three.

The black keys are named in relation to the nearby white keys. They each have two names, known as *enharmonic equivalents.* A black key is named as the *sharp* (♯) of the note to its left, or as the *flat* (♭) of the key to its right. For instance, the black key between the C and D keys is referred to either as C♯ or D♭, depending on the musical context. (For more about sharps, flats, and enharmonic equivalents, see page 17.) With this information, you can name all of the keys on a keyboard. As you experiment with this, you will find that all of the notes with the same name have a sound that differs only because of how low or high they are. That is to say, every A sounds the same, except for the fact that some are low and some are high. This has to do with the mathematical frequencies of the different notes. When you are naming notes at the keyboard and you begin to repeat note names, this is called a new *octave.* At every octave, the position of the note in relation to the surrounding keys is the same. For example, every C is to the left of the group of two black keys, and every F is to the left of the group of three black keys. There is also one special note we must keep track of on the keyboard—the C closest to the middle. We call this note *middle C.*

Middle
C

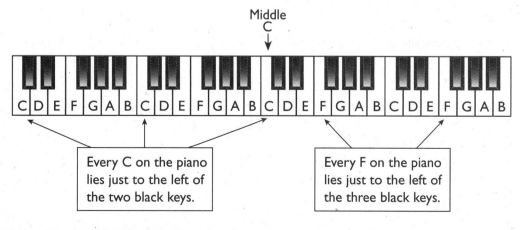

Every C on the piano lies just to the left of the two black keys.

Every F on the piano lies just to the left of the three black keys.

Musical Notation—Pitch

Pitch is the frequency of a note—how high or low it is. When you play the keyboard, the changes in pitch can be heard easily. As you know, each pitch is given a letter name. If you keep these letter names in mind as you play the keyboard, you will quickly learn what these pitches look like on the keyboard. The next step is to understand what they look like on a page of music. In a basic way, learning to read music means making the connection between reading a pitch in the written music and locating it on the keyboard.

Throughout history, different ways of notating music developed so that performers could interpret the correct pitches and rhythms. In Europe, a system was devised that is now used to notate classical music, jazz, and yes, blues. Although blues was originally an oral tradition (meaning it was not written down), nowadays, it helps to be able to read music well. This will allow you to learn music faster and play in all kinds of musical situations.

The Staff

Music is written on a *staff* consisting of five lines. In between each line there is a space.

Treble Clef

In order to show exactly where these staffs, or staves, line up with note names, we use symbols called *clefs*. The *treble clef* 𝄞, also known as *G clef*, circles the G above middle C on the staff. From there, we can figure out the other notes. On the treble-clef staff, the lines are E–G–B–D–F and the spaces are F–A–C–E from bottom (low) to top (high). On keyboard instruments, the notes of the treble clef are typically played with the right hand.

Lines   Spaces

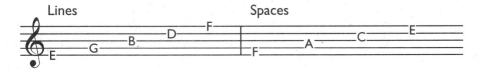

Bass Clef

There is a *bass clef* 𝄢, or *F clef*, for lower-pitched notes. Its dots surround the F below middle C. The lines of the bass-clef staff are G–B–D–F–A, and its spaces are A–C–E–G. The notes of the bass clef are typically played with the left hand.

Lines   Spaces

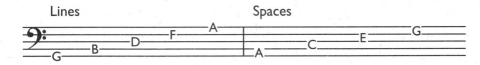

Musical Notation—Time

All music exists in time. The combination of sound and silence gives music its shape. Blues music is based on a steady pulse called the *beat*. In order for musicians to show sound or silence in relation to this beat they use notes and rests.

Note and Rest Values

The *value*, or length, of a note is based on how it relates to the beat. A note that gets one beat is written differently from a note that receives two beats or a half a beat. In written music, a series of note values are used to show length. The longest note (a whole note) is shown as an open ellipse, or *notehead*. To represent a shorter sound, a *stem* is added. To make it shorter still, the notehead is filled in. Finally, *flags* are added to the stem to represent even shorter notes. When these notes are placed on the staff they tell the performer what pitch to play and how long to play it. When referring to the chart to the right, keep in mind that a half note is 1/2 the value of a whole note, a quarter note is 1/4 the value of a whole note, an eighth note is 1/8 the value of a whole note, and a sixteenth note is 1/16 the value of a whole note.

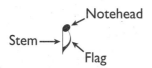

Note Values

Beams and Counting

When eighth notes or sixteenth notes are written next to each other, they are *beamed* together instead of using flags. These notes are always beamed together in a way that shows how the beat is divided.

Beamed eighth notes

Count: 1 & 2 & 3 & 4 &

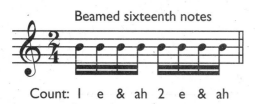

Beamed sixteenth notes

Count: 1 e & ah 2 e & ah

Notice the counting numbers underneath the notes above. Whereas quarter notes are counted "1, 2, 3, 4" on each beat, eighth notes are counted "1-&, 2-&, 3-&, 4-&," and sixteenth notes are counted "1-e-&-ah, 2-e-&-ah, 3-e-&-ah, 4-e-&-ah."

Rests

Just as notes show sound, rests represent silences of varying lengths.

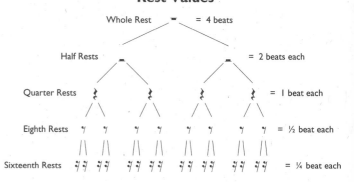

Rest Values

Each rest correlates with a specific note, for example:

Dotted Rhythms

When we want to add value to a note or rest, we can use a *dot*. A dot adds one half of a note's original value. For example, a quarter note is one beat, half of one is one half, so a dotted quarter note is one and a half beats long. Check out some more dotted notes below.

Ties

The value of a note can also be increased using *ties*. Ties are curved lines that connect two or more notes of the same pitch. When playing tied notes, you combine the values of the notes that are tied. Play the first note, and continue to hold it for the length of both (or all) notes. As you will see later, ties are most useful when you want to extend the value of a note over the barline into the next measure.

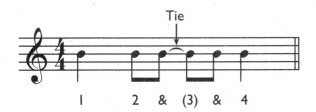

Measures and Barlines

The staff is divided by vertical lines called *barlines*. The space between two barlines is called a *measure*. Measures (sometimes called *bars*) divide music into groups of beats. A *double barline* marks the end of a section or example. The *final barline* signals the end of the piece of music.

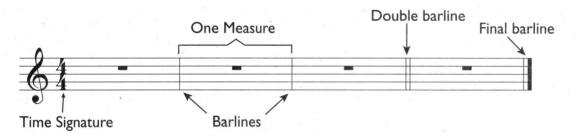

Time Signatures

At the beginning of each piece of music—directly after the clef—is a *time signature*, which contains two numbers, one above the other. The top number tells us how many beats are in each measure. The bottom number indicates what type of note receives one beat. Interpreting the top number is straightforward. If the top number is 2, then there will be two beats, or counts, in each measure. If the top number is 4, then there will be four beats in each measure, and so on.

Interpreting the lower number requires more thought. Think of it as the bottom part of a fraction. Imagine the top number as the number 1. What would you call this fraction if the bottom number was 4 and the top number was 1? You would call it ¼, or a quarter. Think about what type of note has the same name as this fraction and you will know what type of note gets one beat. In this case, it's a quarter note. If the bottom number of the time signature is 2, then the half note would get one beat in each measure. Following are examples of typical time signatures.

$\frac{4}{4}$ = Four beats per measure
$\frac{4}{4}$ = The quarter note ♩ = one beat

$\frac{6}{8}$ = Six beats per measure
$\frac{6}{8}$ = The eighth note ♪ = one beat

$\frac{2}{4}$ = Two beats per measure
$\frac{2}{4}$ = The quarter note ♩ = one beat

$\frac{3}{4}$ = Three beats per measure
$\frac{3}{4}$ = The quarter note ♩ = one beat

Other Important Symbols and Info

Notation is a system of symbols. Once you learn what each of the symbols means, you can interpret them as they appear on the page and start reading music. We've already learned how to interpret the most important musical symbols. Following are some others you need to know.

Repeat Sign

A "thick/thin" double barline with two dots in front of it tells you that you will need to repeat a section of music. Look back in the music to find a repeat symbol facing the opposite way and begin your repeat there. If there is no repeat symbol paired with the first one you encountered, then you should begin your repeat from the very start of the piece.

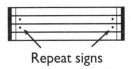

Repeat signs

Slurs

A *slur* is a curved line (⌢) drawn over or under two or more different notes to indicate they are to be played *legato,* or smooth and connected. There should be no break in the sound between these notes. Slurs can look a bit like ties, so be careful when reading them. You will know a tie from a slur because a tie connects two or more of the same note, while a slur connects different notes.

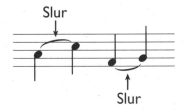

Tempo Markings

Tempo is the speed of a piece of music, and it is indicated at the top of the music in a variety of ways. Sometimes, English terms such as "quickly" or "moderately" are used. Other times, tempo is shown using Italian terms such as the following.

Largo—Very Slow

Adagio—Slow

Andante—Walking Speed

Moderato—moderately

Allegro—Cheerfully

Vivace—Lively

Presto—Quickly

Other pieces of music will indicate tempo using beats per minute (bpm), in which case, it will be shown like below.

♩ = 92

This means that the speed of a quarter note is at 92 beats per minute. You will need a *metronome* (an adjustable time-keeping device) if you want to figure out that exact speed. Sometimes, you can estimate it if you remember that 60 bpm equals one beat per second and 120 bpm equals two beats per second.

Tempos can also change gradually. Italian terms are used for that as well. *Ritardando,* abbreviated *rit.*, indicates a gradual slowing of the tempo. *Accelerando* (*accel.*) calls for a gradual increase in tempo.

Dynamic Markings

Dynamic markings are symbols that tell musicians how loud or soft to perform a particular section of music. Again, Italian terms are used.

Symbol	Italian	English
p	piano	soft
f	forte	loud
mp	mezzo piano	medium soft
mf	mezzo forte	medium loud
pp	pianissimo	very soft
ff	fortissimo	very loud
◁	crescendo	gradually louder
▷	diminuendo	gradually softer

Flats and Sharps

Other symbols you will see when reading music are sharps (♯) and flats (♭), which were introduced on page 10. A sharp raises a pitch by a half step, while a flat lowers a pitch by a half step. Both sharps and flats are known as *accidentals*. On the keyboard, the accidentals are the black keys. The white keys are known as *natural* notes. Flats and sharps are named by their relationship with a natural note. To get from C to C♯, you need to find the note C and go up (to the right) to the very next black key and that will give you C♯. To go from G to G♭, you need to go in the opposite direction (to the left). When sharps and flats are used in written music, they apply only to that exact pitch (not the octave) and for that measure only. If a sharp or flat needs to be canceled, a *natural sign* (♮) will be written. Note that when we call accidentals by name, we say the "sharp," "flat," or "natural" after the note name. When we write them in music, the accidental sign precedes the written note.

Any given key on the piano can have more than one note name. When it does, the two notes are called enharmonic equivalents (introduced on page 10), or notes with the same pitch but different names. For instance, C♯ and D♭ are enharmonically equivalent.

In some cases, white keys can be named using accidentals. Can you locate F♭? It is just below F. But there is no black key there... That means the F♭ is actually the same key as E natural. Other examples are C♭, which is enharmonically equivalent to B, and E♯, which is enharmonically equivalent to F. These different names are used depending on the musical context.

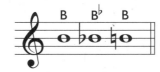

There are also such things as *double flats* (♭♭) and *double sharps* (x). These raise or lower a note by two piano keys. Cx for example is enharmonically equivalent to D. Since it is easier to simply use D, in most situations, that note is simply called D. But in some rare cases, the double sharp is needed in ensure the correct spelling of a chord or melody.

Putting It All Together: The Grand Staff

Most keyboard music is written using the *grand staff,* which is actually two staves joined together with a bracket. The top staff uses the treble clef and the bottom uses the bass clef. And which note is found directly between the two staves? That's right, it's middle C. Middle C has a *ledger line* going through it. Ledger lines are used to show notes above or below the staves. You can use an unlimited number of ledger lines to show very high or low notes on either end of the staff.

Once you understand the grand staff, you must understand how it relates to the keys on the keyboard. Use middle C as a reference point. The higher that a note is written on the grand staff, the higher sounding the pitch (and more to the right on the keyboard). The lower that a note is written on the staff, the lower sounding the pitch (and more to the left on the keyboard).

The Grand Staff

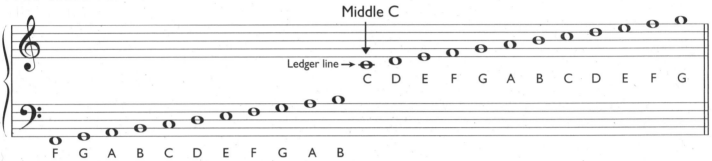

Reading the Grand Staff at the Keyboard

Look at the diagram below. It helps to see how the keyboard relates to the grand staff. The middle of the staff correlates roughly to the middle of the keyboard. Each line or space on the staff corresponds to a key on the keyboard. When the notes move up the page (up and to the right), they do so on the instrument as well. When they move lower on the page, they move lower (to the left) on the keyboard.

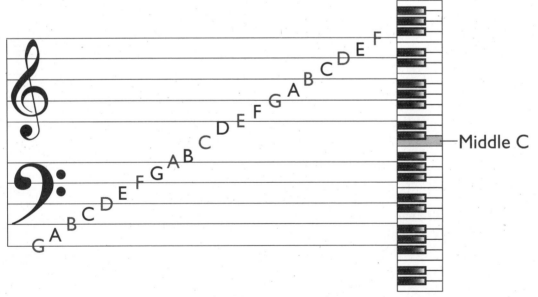

Fingering

Playing specific notes with certain fingers is sometimes required for fluid piano playing. For that reason, the fingers are numbered starting with the thumb as finger number 1, the index finger as number 2, and so on. The finger numbers are the same for both hands.

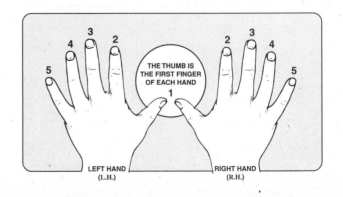

Chapter 2: Basic Music Theory

Music theory helps explain how music works. It gives musicians the fundamental knowledge to understand what makes music sound good to our ears. As a blues player, music theory will give you the foundation for knowledgeable playing, writing, and improvisation. Although most old-time blues players had no formal music theory training, they often learned from other musicians, or figured out the basics of music theory on their own. Even though many blues musicians could not read music, one listen to their playing makes it apparent that they had a deep understanding of how music is put together.

Intervals

One of the most basic concepts in music theory is the *interval*, which is the distance between two notes. It is helpful to see these distances at the keyboard and what they look like on the staff. Each interval also has a unique sound. As you familiarize yourself with how these intervals look, you should also play them on the keyboard and become accustomed to how they sound.

Half Steps and Whole Steps

The smallest intervals are *half steps* and *whole steps*. A half step is the distance between any key on the keyboard and the very next key (black or white). A whole step is equal to two half steps, or two adjacent keys, in either direction.

Perfect and Major Intervals

The distances between notes are identified by both a quality and a number, such as major 2nd, perfect 5th, etc. (Though we may also refer to the 1st as a *unison* and the 8th as an octave.) We'll start by looking at the *major* and *perfect* intervals, and the distances in half steps between the two notes that comprise them (see below). The possible perfect intervals are: perfect unison, perfect 4th, perfect 5th, and perfect octave. The possible major intervals are: major 2nd, major 3rd, major 6th, and major 7th. Notice that a *major 2nd* is the same as a whole step. Don't forget to play all of these intervals on the keyboard to familiarize yourself with how they sound.

Major and Perfect Intervals

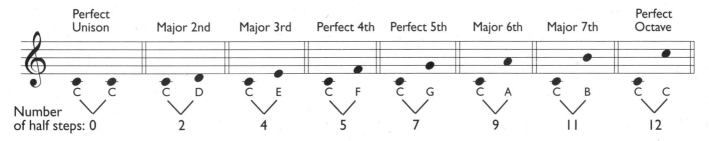

Minor, Diminished, and Augmented Intervals

Using the major and perfect intervals as starting points, you can build *minor, diminished,* and *augmented* intervals. When you lower a major interval by a half step, it becomes a minor interval. The possible minor intervals are: minor 2nd (same as a half step), minor 3rd, minor 6th, and minor 7th. When perfect intervals are made smaller by a half step, the result is a diminished interval. The most common diminished interval is perhaps the diminished

5th. Perfect intervals can also be made larger by increasing the distance between the notes by a half step; these are called augmented intervals. The most common augmented intervals are the augmented 4th (which is the same distance as the diminished 5th) and the augmented 5th. See below for a list of common minor, diminished, and augmented intervals.

Common Minor, Diminished, and Augmented Intervals

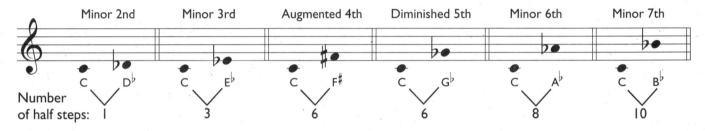

Rare Intervals

When a minor interval is made smaller by a half step, it also becomes diminished. These intervals, such as the diminished 3rd, are rare because there is an easier way to write them. For example, a diminished 3rd sounds the same as a major 2nd but is written differently. Similarly, when major intervals are increased by a half step, they

become augmented intervals and are very rare. The octave and unison can also be diminished or augmented, but this is almost never done in practical music. To make these diminished and augmented intervals, double flats or double sharps are sometimes needed.

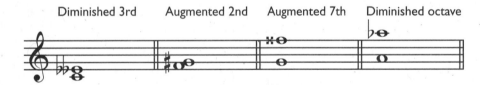

All of the intervals we have been discussing have unique sounds. Play them both *melodically* (one pitch after another) and *harmonically* (both pitches at the same time), and listen to the sound they create. In order to remember what these intervals sound like, you can reference popular songs that start with those same intervals (see the chart

at the top of the next page). As you practice, experiment by forming intervals starting with any note on the piano. Seeing, playing, constructing, and hearing intervals prepares a musician to do more sophisticated things like build chords and learn music by ear.

Interval	Abbreviation	Popular Song
Minor 2nd	m2	The theme from the movie *Jaws*
Major 2nd	M2	"Happy Birthday"
Minor 3rd	m3	"Greensleeves"
Major 3rd	M3	"When the Saints Go Marching In"
Perfect 4th	P4	"Here Comes the Bride"
Aug. 4th/Dim. 5th	A4/d5	"Maria" from the musical *West Side Story*
Perfect 5th	P5	The main theme from the movie *Star Wars*
Minor 6th	m6	The theme from the movie *Love Story*
Major 6th	M6	NBC network theme
Minor 7th	m7	"There's a Place for Us" from *West Side Story*
Major 7th	M7	"Don't Know Why" by Norah Jones
Perfect Octave	P8	"Somewhere Over the Rainbow"

Scales

The musical *scale* is one of the most important concepts in all of music. A scale is a collection of notes on which a melody, chord progression, or improvisation can be based. Scales are basically a series of notes in alphabetical order, and each scale has a specific organization of half steps and whole steps that gives it its unique sound.

Scale Degrees

Scales may consist of five, six, seven, or more notes. These notes are each given a number called a *scale degree*. Below is the C Major scale with its scale degrees numbered.

C Major Scale

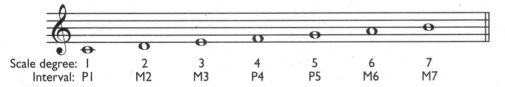

These scale degrees can be referred to by their interval from the lowest note of the scale (also known as the *root*). The scale above includes a perfect unison (P1), major 2nd, major 3rd, perfect 4th, perfect 5th, major 6th, and major 7th.

Scale degrees can also have names that help to identify their place in the scale. They are: *tonic* (root), *supertonic* (2), *mediant* (3), *subdominant* (4), *dominant* (5), *submediant* (6), and *leading tone* (7). While some of these are not used often, the words "tonic" and "dominant" come up over and over again in the study of music.

Major Scales

Major scales are the most common scales in music. They consist of seven notes (not including the repeated root note at the top) and have a specific formula of whole steps and half steps that you should become familiar with. This formula is: whole step–whole step–half step–whole step–whole step–whole step–half step. You can memorize this by thinking "whole–whole–half–whole–whole–whole–half." Chant it aloud a few times, and you'll probably have it down. See below for how the notes of the C Major scale correlate to this formula.

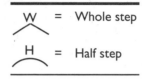

W = Whole step

H = Half step

C Major Scale

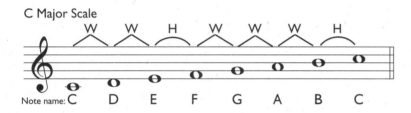

Note name: C D E F G A B C

W W H W W W H

Using this formula (or the list of intervals on page 21), you can build a major scale starting from any note. When any note other than C is the root of the scale, accidentals will be needed. Some major scales will require sharps and some will need flats; no major scales use both. Remember to keep the notes in alphabetical order as you build the scales and you will be able to determine what accidentals are needed.

Let's build a scale starting on F. What is a whole step above F? The answer is G. Next, we need another whole step, which gives us an A (remember, in the musical alphabet, after G you go back to A). Next, we need a half step. However, from A to B is a whole step, so we need to lower the B to a B♭ to give us the half step. If we called this A♯, we would not be proceeding alphabetically, because we would be repeating A. The complete scale is: F–G–A–B♭–C–D–E–F. For this and another example (the D Major Scale), take a look below.

F Major Scale

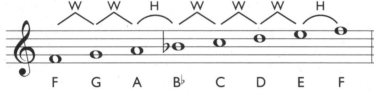

F G A B♭ C D E F

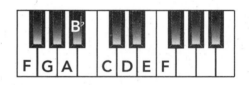

D Major Scale

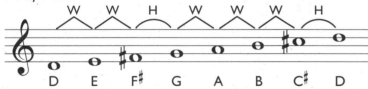

D E F♯ G A B C♯ D

In order to play the major scales fluidly, you need to use the correct fingerings. On the next page, you will find all 12 major scales and their proper fingerings. Note that there are some spots where the thumb passes under the other fingers in the right hand (see * in the C Major scale) and where the 3rd finger crosses over the 1st finger in the left hand (see ** in the C Major scale). Try practicing the hands separately and together.

The 12 Major Scales

All 12 major scales are shown below. You should learn how to play each of these scales ascending and descending with both hands.

While it is important to learn all the keys, the most common blues keys are C, G, D, A, E, F, and B♭.

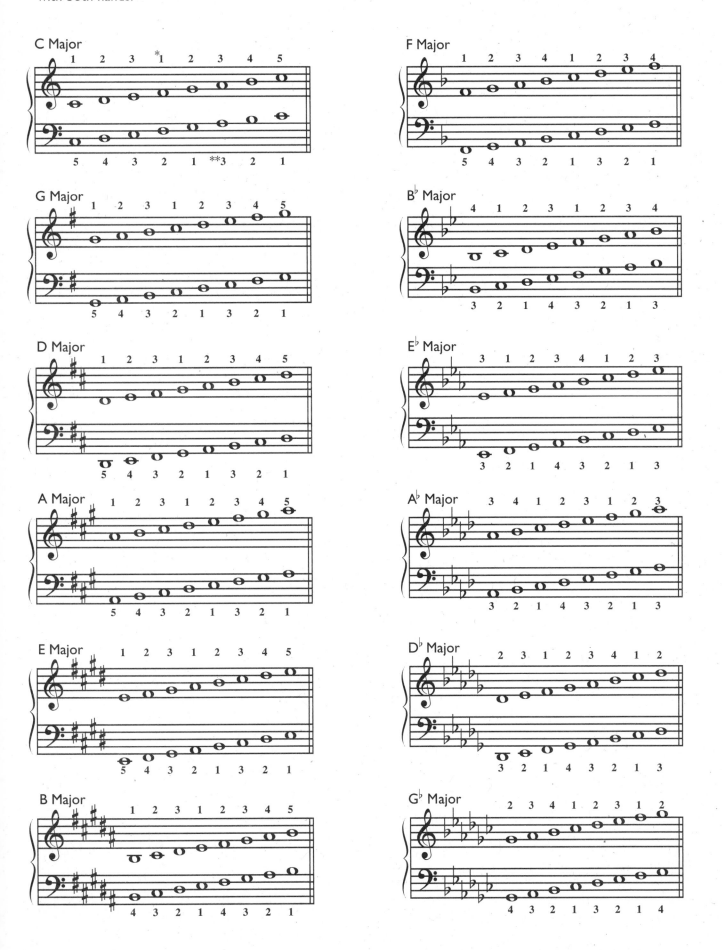

Modes of the Major Scale

In order to understand some of the other important scales in music, we need to learn about the *modes,* which are derived directly from the major scale. These are sometimes called church modes, or Greek modes, because they were used extensively in ancient music and medieval chant. All of the modes are named for places in the ancient Greek world. All of the seven modes contain the exact same notes as the major scale from which they are derived. The notes even occur in the same order. The only things that change are the starting and ending points. For example, the Dorian mode (of the C Major scale) consists of the same notes as the C Major scale but runs from D to D rather than from C to C. Let's look at the others.

Modes of the Major Scale

The **Ionian** mode (same as the major scale) is built on the root of the major scale.

Ionian Mode

The **Dorian** mode is built on the 2nd scale degree of the major scale.

Dorian Mode

The **Phrygian** mode starts on the 3rd scale degree of the major scale.

Phrygian Mode

The **Lydian** mode is built on the 4th scale degree of the major scale.

Lydian Mode

The **Mixolydian** mode is built on the 5th scale degree of the major scale.

Mixolydian Mode

The **Aeolian** mode is built on the 6th scale degree of the major scale (identical to the *natural minor scale,* see next page).

Aeolian Mode

The **Locrian** mode is built on the 7th scale degree of the major scale.

Locrian Mode

Notice the Ionian mode is the same as the major scale. Musicians sometimes ask, "Why do we need modes?" The answer is, because each mode has a unique and interesting sound. The Dorian mode has a minor 3rd and a major 6th. The Phrygian mode has a minor 2nd, minor 3rd, minor 6th, and minor 7th. These lead to interesting melodies and harmonies that can greatly enrich any song. Not only were the modes used extensively in ancient and medieval music, they also came to be used in folk music, jazz, and modern classical music. They are even used from time to time in the blues. Over the course of music history, two of these modes came to be used more than all the others. The Ionian, which we already learned is the same as the major scale, and the Aeolian, which is the same as the natural minor scale. Take a look at the Aeolian mode—it has a major 2nd, minor 3rd, perfect 4th, perfect 5th, minor 6th, and minor 7th. It consists of the following scale degrees: $1-2-\flat 3-4-5-\flat 6-\flat 7$. This gives it a darker sound than the major scale.

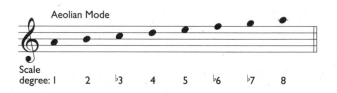

Aeolian Mode

Scale degree: 1 2 $\flat$3 4 5 $\flat$6 $\flat$7 8

Minor Scales

Natural Minor

The Aeolian mode is also known as the natural minor scale. Like the major scale, it has a specific configuration of whole and half steps, which is as follows: whole step–half step–whole step–whole step–half step–whole step–whole step. In the example below, you can see how the natural minor scale lines up with the major scale from which it is derived. There are also two variations of the minor scale, which we'll look at momentarily.

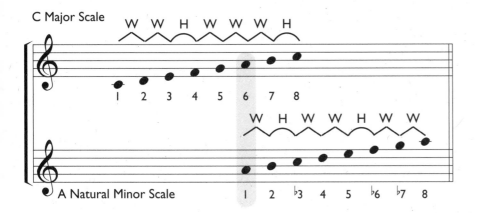

C Major Scale

A Natural Minor Scale

Harmonic Minor

The *harmonic minor scale* is named as such because of its use in harmony. It differs from the natural minor scale in that it has a ♮7. The interval between root and 7th in a natural minor scale is a minor 7th, but the interval between root and 7th in a harmonic minor scale is a major 7th. "Raising" the 7th creates a leading tone in the scale, just like the 7th degree in the major scale. This allows for interesting harmonies when chord progressions are made using this scale. The scale degrees for the harmonic minor scale are: 1–2–♭3–4–5–♭6–7.

A Harmonic Minor Scale

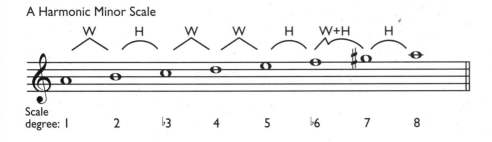

Scale degree: 1   2   ♭3   4   5   ♭6   7   8

W+H = One and a half steps

Melodic Minor

The *melodic minor scale* developed because of a desire to write more varied melodies in the minor tonality. In the melodic minor scale, both the 6th and 7th scale degrees are raised from their natural minor form, but only when ascending. When descending, the melodic minor scale takes the same form as the natural minor scale. So the formula for the melodic minor scale is 1–2–♭3–4–5–6–7 when ascending and 1–2–♭3–4–5–♭6–♭7 when descending.

A Melodic Minor Scale

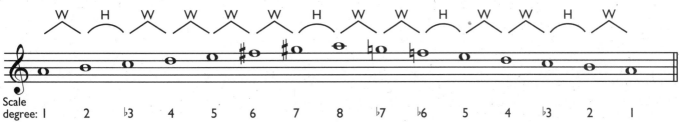

Scale degree: 1   2   ♭3   4   5   6   7   8   ♭7   ♭6   5   4   ♭3   2   1

Key Signatures

If we were to write out all of the major scales, we would see that some of them require many accidentals. For example, the C♯ Major scale has seven sharps; if we follow the order of whole steps and half steps, we get the notes C♯, D♯, E♯, F♯, G♯, A♯, and B♯. That's a lot of sharps! If you had to write or read those sharps in front of every note in an entire song, it would be cumbersome and difficult.

C♯ Major Scale

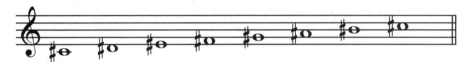

Instead of writing the sharps over and over again, we can say the music is in the *key* of C♯ Major. That means that C♯ is the tonic, or *tonal center*, and the music will mostly use the C♯ Major scale. To show this key, we will need a *key signature*, or a "list" of what notes will be sharp (or flat) for the whole piece.

C♯ Major Scale with Key Signature

Key signatures are written directly to the right of a clef on a piece of music. While key signatures can be made up of sharps or flats, they never include both at the same time. The accidentals in the key signature apply throughout the entire piece and to notes in all octaves; the only exceptions are when a natural sign or new key signature appear in the music. Even keys with one or two accidentals use key signatures, such as the key of F. The F Major scale requires one flat, B♭. Therefore, the key signature for F has one flat, B♭. That means that all the Bs in that song are played as B♭ unless they have a natural sign in front of them. There is even a key with no sharps or flats, and that's the key of C Major.

Relative Minor

Minor keys are written using the same key signatures as major keys, but the key signature for C Minor is not the same as the key signature for C Major. The key signature for A Minor is the same as the key signature of C Major. That's because A Minor is the *relative minor* of C Major. When keys are relative, it means they share the same key signature. They do so because they share the same notes.

Remember, A Natural Minor is the Aeolian mode derived from the C Major scale, and it starts on the 6th scale degree of C Major. Each major key has a relative minor that can be found by counting up to its 6th scale degree. For example, the 6th scale degree of the D Major scale is B, so B Minor is the relative minor of D Major.

D Major Scale

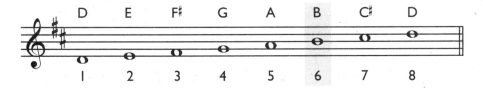

B Minor Scale—Relative Minor of D Major

Parallel Minor

Though C Minor is not the relative minor of C Major, it is the *parallel minor*. That means both scales share the same root. While their key signatures are quite different, they both begin and end on C.

C Major Scale

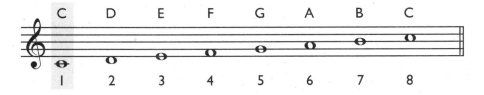

C Minor Scale—Parallel Minor of C Major

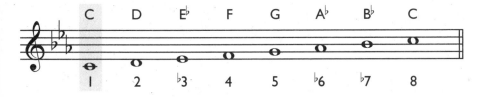

The Circle of 5ths

If there is one chart that clearly shows the relationships between all of the keys, it is the *circle of 5ths,* which depicts the keys around a circle. As you go clockwise around the circle, the keys ascend in perfect 5ths, and with each new key, one sharp is added to the key signature. As you go counterclockwise around the circle, the keys descend in perfect 5ths, adding one flat at a time to each new key signature. You could also view the counterclockwise motion as ascending in perfect 4ths, as a perfect 4th is an *inverted* perfect 5th. (This means the distance is measured backward, starting from the top note.) At the top of the circle is the key of C, with no sharps or flats. On the right side are the sharp keys: G (one sharp), D (two sharps), A (three sharps), and so on. On the left-hand side are the flat keys: F, B♭, E♭, etc. At the bottom are the keys with the most accidentals and the point where you must change over from sharps to flats in order to continue around the circle. The keys at the bottom have both sharp and flat forms, which have different names but sound the same. These are known as *enharmonic key signatures.*

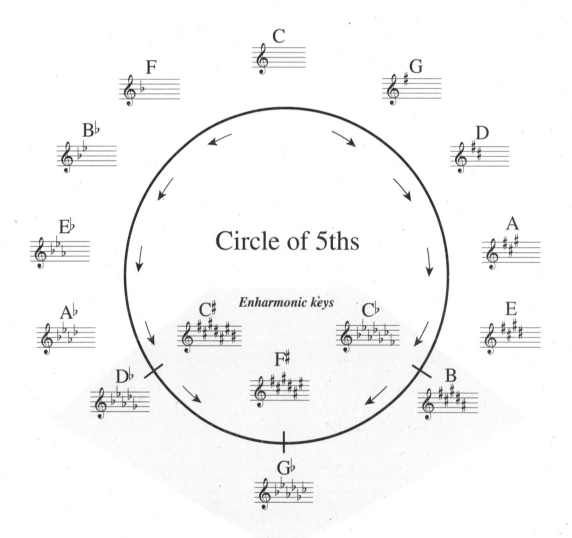

As you learn more about music, it is always a good idea to revisit the circle of 5ths. Each time you do, you'll discover new and interesting relationships among the keys.

Chapter 3: Harmony

Introduction to Triads

One of the truly great things about keyboard instruments is their ability to play *harmony,* or more than one note at the same time. When three or more notes are played simultaneously, the result is a *chord.* There are a variety of chords, from simple three-note chords known as *triads* to far more complex chords consisting of many more notes. There are four types of triads: *major, minor, diminished,* and *augmented.*

Constructing Triads

Triads are three-note chords that form the basis of many blues songs. Triads are made up of 3rds "stacked" one on top of another (done by taking every other note in a scale—for instance, the root, 3rd, and 5th of a major scale). Whether these 3rds are major 3rds, minor 3rds, or a combination of both depends on the type of triad. If you simultaneously play the root, 3rd, and 5th of a C Major scale, you will be playing a C Major triad. All triads have a root, 3rd and 5th; the qualities of these different chord tones depend on the quality of the triad.

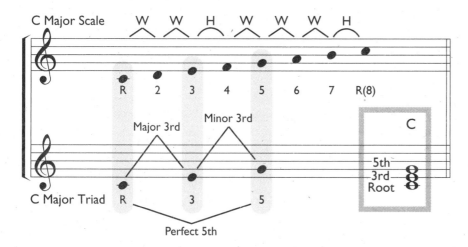

Major Triads

All major triads have the same intervals. Starting with the root, the next note is a major 3rd, and this is followed by a perfect 5th (which is also a minor 3rd above the 3rd of the chord). If you follow this formula, you can build a major triad on top of any note.

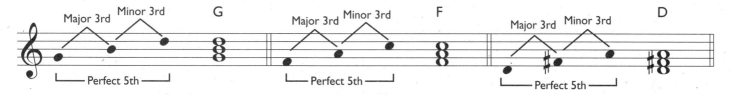

Major triads are usually just called "major chords." Chords can also be indicated using *chord symbols* written above the staff. The symbol for a major chord is a capital letter that is the same as the name of the root of the chord. For example, the chord symbol for a C Major chord is written as "C." Try to play and build the triads below. Look at the fingerings, and listen to the sound of each chord to be sure you are getting the correct notes.

Minor Triads

The intervals in the minor triad are root, minor 3rd, and perfect 5th (1–♭3–5). Minor chords are written with a variety of symbols; the most common (using A as the root) are Amin, Am, or A-. In this book, you will see the first. Take a look at the example below to see how the minor chord is made from the minor scale.

A Natural Minor Scale

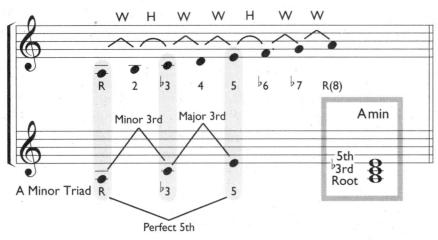

Diminished Triads

As you may remember from our look at intervals, to diminish something means to make it smaller. Diminished chords are similar to minor chords except the 5th is lowered by a half step. The resulting formula is root, minor 3rd, and diminished 5th (1–♭3–♭5). Diminished chords are shown by the symbols Bdim or B°. In this book, you will see Bdim. Below is a C Minor triad followed by a C Diminished triad. Notice that the only difference between them is the ♭5th in the diminished chord.

C Minor Triad

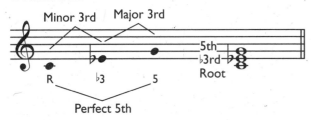

C Diminished Triad

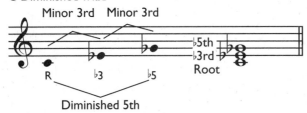

Augmented Triads

Augmented chords are similar to major chords except the 5th is raised by a half step. That makes the formula for augmented chords: root, major 3rd, and augmented 5th (1–3–#5). The symbols for augmented chords are Gaug or G+. In this book, you will see Gaug. Both augmented and diminished chords are less common than minor and major chords, but they do have unique qualities and can be used to create colorful-sounding music. Let's compare a C Major triad to a C Augmented triad.

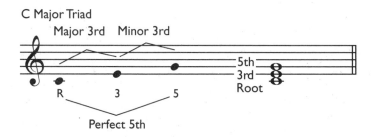

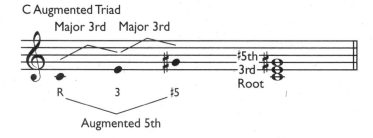

Triad Inversions

So far, we've looked at triads in *root position,* meaning the root is on the bottom of the chord. Triads can also be *inverted* by placing the 3rd or 5th on the bottom. If you reorder the triad so the 3rd is on the bottom, it is in *1st* inversion; if you reorder it so the 5th is on the bottom, then the chord is in *2nd inversion.* These inversions change the sound of the chord and allow for smoothly connected chord progressions.

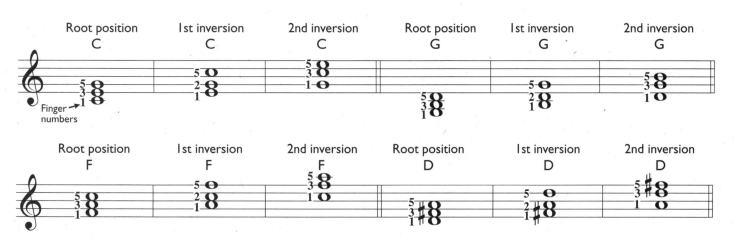

It's a good idea to practice playing all of your triads and their inversions in every key. Try playing: C and its inversions, Cmin and its inversions, Cdim and its inversions, and Caug with its inversions. Then, move around the circle of 5ths, or by half-steps, to practice this in all 12 keys.

7th Chords

To add more color and interest to a chord, you must add more notes. Since chords are built by stacking 3rds, the next possible note that can be added to a triad is a 7th above the root. This creates a four-note chord consisting of root, 3rd, 5th, and 7th. Since these chords contain a 7th above the root, we call them 7th chords.

Dominant 7th Chords

Although there are several types of 7th chords, the most common is the *dominant 7th*. To build a dominant 7th chord, you will need a root, major 3rd, perfect 5th, and minor 7th (1–3–5–♭7). Basically, it's constructed by adding the interval of a minor 7th to a major triad. In the blues, dominant 7ths are used frequently. Since it is the most common type of 7th chord, dominant 7ths are sometimes simply called "seventh," or "seven," chords. This is reflected in their symbol which adds the number 7 to the letter name of the chord's root; for example, C7.

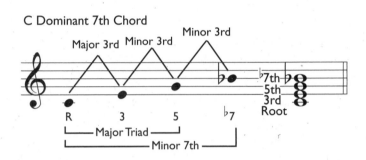

Following is an exercise to help you practice building and playing dominant 7th chords. Try it with both hands.

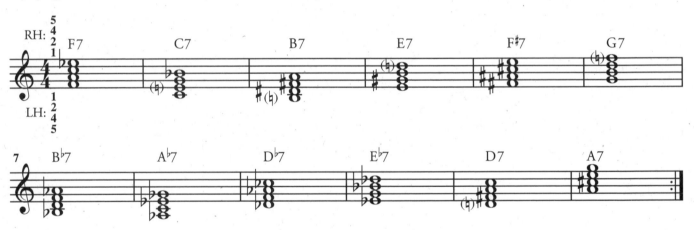

Major 7th Chords

While the dominant 7th chord is by far the most commonly used 7th chord in the blues, other types are used occasionally to add harmonic color and interest. The *major 7th* chord is built with a root, major 3rd, perfect 5th, and major 7th (1–3–5–7). It's like adding a major 7th interval to major triad. It has a bright, pleasant sound and can be represented with the following chord symbols: CMaj7, Cmaj7, and C△7. Occasionally, you will see it listed as CM7, but that can be confusing, since it's often hard to tell whether the "M" is upper or lowercase in handwritten music (Cm7 is one of the symbols for the C Minor 7th chord). In this book, we will use CMaj7.

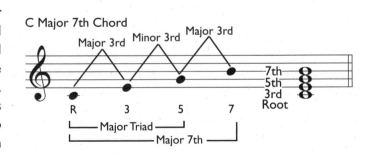

Minor 7th Chords

If you add a minor 7th interval to a minor triad, the result is a *minor 7th* chord. The intervals in this chord are root, minor 3rd, perfect 5th, and minor 7th (1–♭3–5–♭7). It is used often in many styles of music, including the blues, and can be represented by the symbols Cm7, C-7, or Cmin7. In this book, you will see Cmin7.

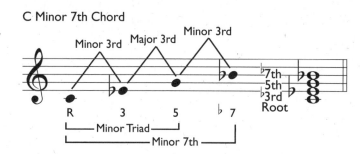

Half-Diminished 7th Chords

Just as we added 7ths to minor and major triads, we can also add a minor 7th interval to a diminished triad to get a *half-diminished 7th* chord. The intervals in this chord are root, minor 3rd, diminished 5th, and minor 7th (1–♭3–♭5–♭7). The half-diminished chord is not used very often in blues music, but when it is, you will know it by the symbols C⌀7, C-7(♭5), Cm7(♭5), or Cmin7♭5. In this book, you will see Cmin7♭5.

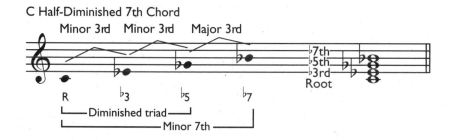

Fully Diminished 7th Chords

There is another type of 7th chord built on top of a diminished triad: the *fully diminished 7th* chord, known also as, simply, the *diminished 7th* chord. The intervals in this chord are root, minor 3rd, diminished 5th, and diminished 7th (1–♭3–♭5–♭♭7). This chord is made by placing a diminished 7th interval on top of a diminished triad. Remember, a diminished 7th is one half step smaller than a minor 7th. For some chords, a diminished 7th interval will require double flats. The symbols for fully diminished 7th chords are Cdim7 and C°7. In this book, we will use Cdim7.

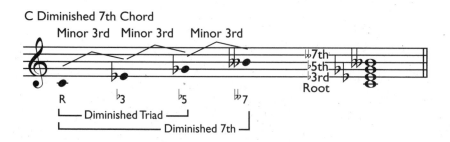

Other 7th Chords

It's fun to think about adding any of the possible 7ths to any of the triads even if these chords are rarely used. If you add a minor 7th to an augmented triad, the result is an augmented 7th chord (1–3–$\sharp$5–$\flat$7), or Caug7. This chord is sometimes heard in jazz. How about adding a major 7th to an augmented triad? The result is a major 7th with a sharp 5th (1–3–$\sharp$5–7), or CMaj7$\sharp$5; this sounds like a slightly unusual major chord. There is also a such thing as a minor-major 7th chord, which is a minor triad with a major 7th (1–$\flat$3–5–7) or CminMaj7. This is a cool chord to use as a final chord for any song in a minor key. Here is another interesting possibility. Take a diminished chord and add a major 7th (1–$\flat$3–$\flat$5–7). This is a truly unusual, but rich sounding chord that could be represented by the chord symbol CdimMaj7.

7th Chord Inversions

7th chords can be inverted just like triads. The difference is that while triads have two inversions, 7th chords have three. When you space these inversions out between two hands, you can "open up" the *voicing*, or configuration of notes, to leave some extra space between the notes (these are called *open voicings*). When chords are written in their inversion the bottom note is shown in the chord symbol by adding a slash and the name of the bass note to the right of the chord symbol, such as C7/E or Dmin7/A. These are known as *slash chords*.

So, if the root of a 7th chord is in the bass, the chord is in root position. If the 3rd is in the bass, the chord is in 1st inversion. If the 5th is in the bass, the chord is in 2nd inversion. And if the 7th is in the bass, the chord is in *3rd inversion*.

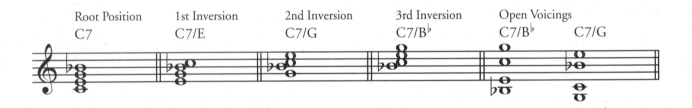

Exercise

Try playing the 7th chords below. Read them carefully, and pay attention to their unique sounds.

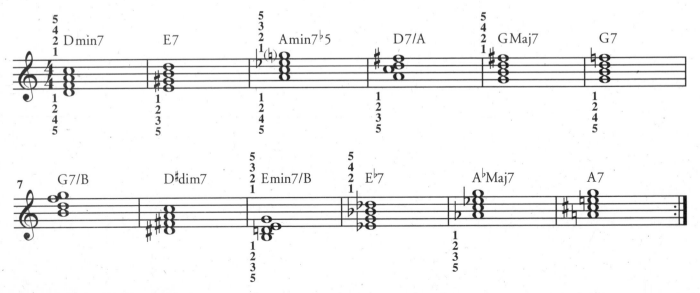

Chord Progressions

Harmony in songs is made up of chords that move from one to another. This is called a *chord progression*.

Assigning Numbers to Chords

In order to make sense of chord progressions, we assign numbers to chords based on which scale degree is their root. If we look at the major scale, we can build a triad on each of the seven scale degrees using only the notes in the major scale. The result is seven different chords—three major triads, three minor triads, and one diminished triad. We give these chords Roman numerals—uppercase if they are major, and lowercase if they are minor or diminished. For the diminished triad, we must also add the diminished symbol (°). This harmonic system is known as *diatonic harmony* (diatonic means belonging to a scale) because only the notes of one particular scale are used to build the chords.

Roman Numeral Review

I or i	1	V or v	5
II or ii	2	VI or vi	6
III or iii	3	VII or vii	7
IV or iv	4		

Diatonic Triads

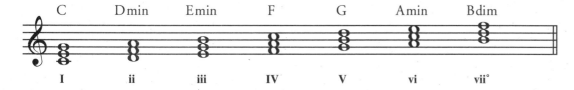

7th chords can also be built on each of the seven scale degrees. Following are the diatonic 7th chords in the key of C.

Diatonic 7th Chords

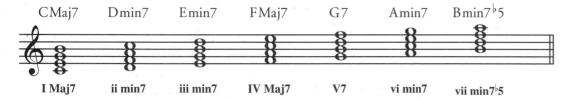

Tonic and Dominant Chords

Traditionally, chords have functions based on the way they work in a chord progression. Chords that give the feeling of the home key, or tonal center, are known as *tonic chords*. The tonic chords are I, iii, and vi. (Do not confuse this with the other names and functions these chords have—mediant, leading tone, etc.—what we are discussing here are just general categories.) The most important of the tonic chords is I, which is the true tonic chord and shares the name of the key (for instance, the C Major chord is the I, the true tonic chord, in the key of C Major). The iii and vi chords share certain qualities with the I chord—and hint at it—but they do not quite have the solid feeling of "home" as the I chord.

There are also two dominant chords, V and vii°, with V as the more important of the two. Dominant chords are at the opposite end of the tonal spectrum from tonic chords. They are the point of most tension in a chord progression, and they wish to resolve to the point of least tension, the tonic. The axis of tonic and dominant is what provides the basis for our harmonic system. While you can create chord progressions with only tonic and dominant chords, more interesting progressions make use of subdominant chords to help the progression move between the tonic and dominant.

Subdominant Chords

Subdominant chords help produce a smooth transition between tonic and dominant. The two subdominant chords based on the major scale are the ii and IV chords. In the blues, the IV chord is the subdominant chord of choice, while in jazz, it is the ii chord.

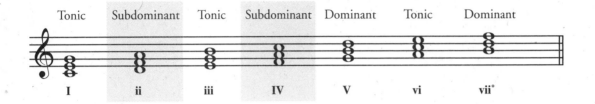

Building Progressions

Many common chord progressions, including a basic blues progression, make use of the three *primary chords:* I (tonic), IV (subdominant), and V (dominant). The most basic progressions move from I to IV to V and back to I. It is also very common to use V7 in place of the V chord. Using inversions, 7th chords, and substitute chords adds color.

Basic Chord Progression

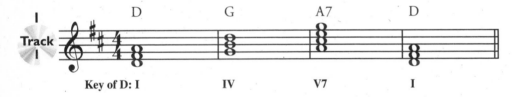

In many songs, the progression of chords is based on the circle of 5ths. Take a look at the modified version of the circle of 5ths to the right.

See how the chords are placed around the circle? Progressions can be based on the counterclockwise motion around the circle. A *retrogression* is the reverse of this counterclockwise direction, or in other words, clockwise. Some progressions use all of the chords and some only use a few. Many also make use of inversions and other substitutions. When motion around the circle of 5ths is obvious in a set of chords, we call it a *circle progression* (see top of next page).

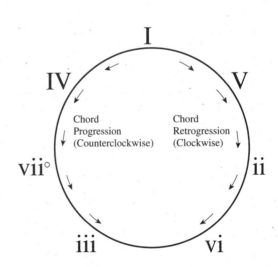

Circle Progression

In rock, blues, and other styles, the tonic to subdominant to dominant motion is reversed from time to time creating an interesting relaxing effect. When this happens the chords begin to move in the opposite direction around the circle of 5ths, usually for a moment, and then back the other way to complete the progression. Following is an example of this type of chord retrogression.

Chord Retrogression

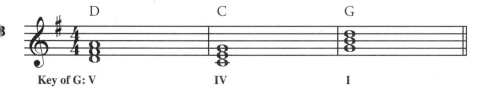

Reading from Lead Sheets

While writing and reading music on the grand staff is very accurate, it can also be cumbersome and, at times, difficult to read quickly. There is another way to write out songs using the performer's knowledge of chords and a bit of improvisation to get it to sound right. This type of music shorthand is called a *lead sheet*. In lead sheet notation, the keyboardist reads only one staff of music on which the melody is written. Above it, the chord symbols are written. If you know how to construct the chords and read the melody, you can create your own version of the song with your own chord voicings or accompaniment. Take a good look at the lead sheet below, and try to play the chords in the left hand and the melody in the right.

D.S., D.C., and Coda

There are various words and symbols that direct the performer to skip to different locations in the written score. These symbols allow the composer to write out all of the information only once. By using a lead sheet, repeats, and the symbols below, you can often get a full song on one page of music.

Symbol	Italian Term	English Definition
D.C.	Da Capo	Repeat from the beginning
D.S.	Dal Segno	Repeat from the sign :‖
Fine	Fine	The end
⊕	Coda	An added ending

The terms above can be used together to create an arrangement of the music written on the page. *D.C. al Fine* means go back to the beginning and end at the word "Fine." *D.S. al Coda* means go back to the sign 𝄋 and play until you reach the coda sign—then, skip to the coda sign at the end of the piece to play the ending. Try playing through the lead sheet below.

Chapter 4: Blusic Theory

Blue Notes

What gives the blues its truly recognizable sound? There are a number of things—including specific note choices, chord progressions, and scales—that help place songs in the blues genre. This chapter is called "Blusic Theory" (perhaps this term will catch on) because it's dedicated to the music theory that applies specifically to the blues. The most important of these ideas are the *blue notes*. No matter what chord progression or groove is played behind a blues song, you can always tell if a song is bluesy because of its tonality or mood. To achieve this mood, you must use blue notes. The blue notes are located near the 3rd, 5th, and 7th of the major scale. These blue notes are actually in between the keys on the piano, meaning they are outside of our normal tuning system. Singers, harmonica players, and guitarists can bend their notes to get close to these blue notes. This gives a performance an ambiguous tonality and a bluesy sound. Obviously, we can't bend notes on the piano, so pianists have developed other ways to hint at the blue notes. These techniques will be explored further as we look at the different styles of blues piano.

C Major Scale With Blue Notes

Cultural Origins of the Blue Notes

Much of what has come to define the blues style comes from the blending of two cultures in the American South. As slavery came to dominate the economy of the South before the Civil War, Africans were forced from their homes in West Africa to work on the plantations. They took with them their culture, including their music. One trait of West African music is the use of tonalities that are "out of tune" by European standards. Influenced by Arabic music, West African scales include *microtones,* or intervals less than a half step. As these traditions merged with music of the European-based culture of the American South, a new sound developed that combined both traditions. One musical result of this cultural blending are blue notes and the blues scales.

Pentatonic Scales

Blues melodies can be made from several collections of notes. One of the standard choices is the *pentatonic scale*, which is a five-note scale. This contrasts with the major and minor scales, which have seven notes.

Major Pentatonic

The standard pentatonic scales can be built by leaving notes out of the major or minor scales. Using the major scale, you can build a *major pentatonic scale* by leaving out the 4th and 6th scale degrees. So the formula for a major pentatonic scale is: 1–2–3–5–6. Since it is built from the major scale, this has a distinctly major sound.

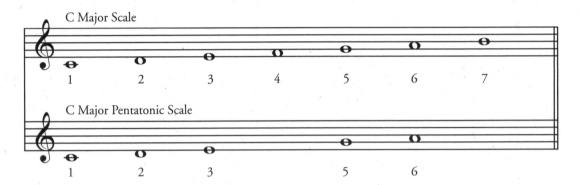

Minor Pentatonic

Another pentatonic scale is the *minor pentatonic*. There are two ways to look at how this scale is built. If you start with the natural minor scale and leave out the 2nd and 6th scale degrees, you will have the formula for the minor pentatonic scale: 1–♭3–4–5–♭7. Also, if you were to play the major pentatonic scale starting with the 6th scale degree, you would be playing its relative minor pentatonic scale. For example, if you play a C Major Pentatonic scale (C–D–E–G–A) starting with the A note, you will be playing the A Minor Pentatonic scale (A–C–D–E–G).

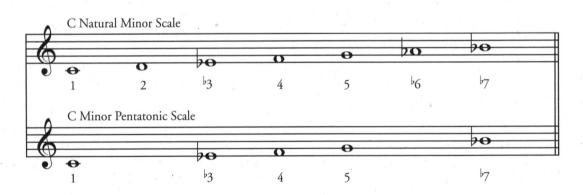

The Minor Pentatonic as a Relative of the Major

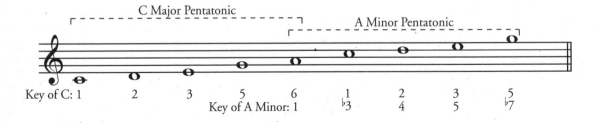

The Minor Blues Scale

The *minor blues scale* is a well-known and very useful scale that contains all of the blue notes. It can be thought of as a minor pentatonic scale with an added ♭5. The formula for the scale is: 1–♭3–4–♭5–5–♭7. Since it contains all of the important blue notes (functionally, these would be the ♭3, ♭5, and ♭7), it will give you a very bluesy sound in both major and minor keys. To play the blues, you will need to know this scale in all 12 keys.

A Minor Blues Scale   D Minor Blues Scale

G Minor Blues Scale   C Minor Blues Scale

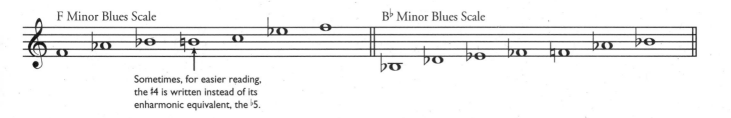

F Minor Blues Scale   B♭ Minor Blues Scale

Sometimes, for easier reading, the ♯4 is written instead of its enharmonic equivalent, the ♭5.

E♭ Minor Blues Scale   A♭ Minor Blues Scale

C♯ Minor Blues Scale   F♯ Minor Blues Scale

B Minor Blues Scale   E Minor Blues Scale

Minor Blues Scale Melody

Take a look at the melody below. It's written using the
C Minor Blues scale.

The Major Blues Scale

The *major blues scale* can be thought of as a major
pentatonic scale with an added ♭3. Its formula is: 1–2–♭3–
3–5–6. Because of the ♭3 blue note, this scale can also be
used to create bluesy sounding melodies. Some blues tunes
even make use of both the minor and major blues scales.
After playing the scale below, try it in all 12 keys.

C Major Blues Scale

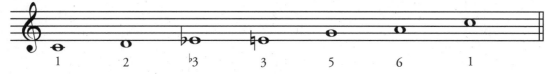

Major Blues Scale Melody

The melody below is built on the C Major Blues scale.

The 12-Bar Blues

While blues songs can have many different forms or chord progressions, the most common is a 12-measure chord progression called the *12-bar blues* ("bar" being another word for measure). It is made up of three 4-bar phrases. Melodically, the second phrase is usually a repeat, or echo, of the first phrase, but over new chords. The final phrase is a response to the first two.

Basic 12-Bar Blues

In its most basic form, the 12-bar blues contains only three chords. In any key, these chords are known by their numbers I, IV, and V. The traditional form follows:

- Four measures of the I chord
- Two measures of the IV chord
- Two measures of the I chord
- One measure of the V chord
- One measure of the IV chord
- Two measures of the I chord

Each time through the 12-bar progression is called a *chorus*. The progression is repeated many times to create an entire song. See the example on the next page.

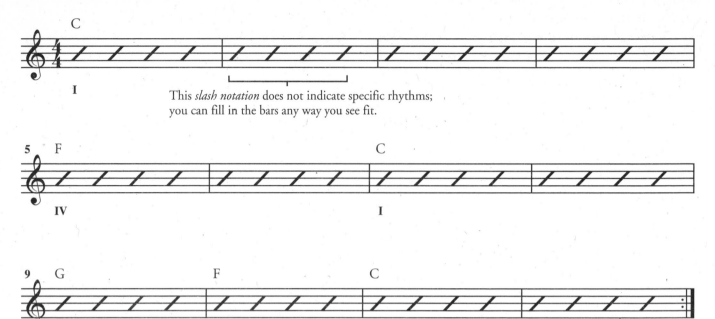

This *slash notation* does not indicate specific rhythms; you can fill in the bars any way you see fit.

12-Bar Blues with Standard Substitutions

In any chord progression, chords can be added or substituted for other chords based on the standard principals of harmony. Over the decades, many standard substitutions have developed for blues songs. The most important is that 7th chords can be substituted for the simple triads seen above. The IV and V chords can also be added in more places to produce more motion in the progression. See below.

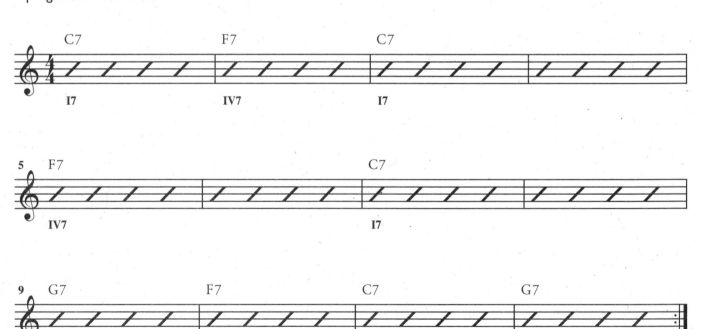

"Simply the Blues" is our first full song. It features two choruses of 12-bar blues in C Major. The first chorus has a steady half-note pulse and single-line melody, while the second has a quarter-note pulse and a harmonized melody. Practice playing both hands separately and then putting them together. Chord symbols are also provided if you would like to try and develop your own accompaniment.

Track 7 Simply the Blues

Blues Lyric Structure

All blues was originally developed as a vocal music. To fully understand the 12-bar blues form, it's important to understand the lyric structure of the blues. The main idea of any blues song is to tell a story or communicate a feeling. In a blues, the first line makes a statement, which is then repeated over new chords. The final line is a response to the first two. This creates a three-part form, which we can refer to as *AAB*, with each line sung over 4 bars of music. The response (B) often rhymes with the call phrases (A). Below are two lyric examples in the style of early blues legend Robert Johnson.

Example 1
A *I walked to the river, fell down on the ground*
A *I walked to the river, fell down on the ground*
B *Asked the lord a question, but I didn't hear a sound*

Example 2
A *Come on, honey, don't you want a ride?*
A *Come on, baby, don't you want a ride?*
B *To that same old place, down by the oceanside*

Following is a blues lyric based on the melody from page 42.

Lonesome Blues

Transposing the Blues Progression

The basic 12-bar blues progression can be played in any of the 12 keys. As a blues musician, you should practice playing the chords in all of the keys. It's a good idea to use the circle of 5ths to guide the order in which you practice them. No matter what key you are in, the relationships among the chords stays the same. Below are some examples of the progression transposed to two different keys: F and G.

12-Bar Blues in the Key of F

12-Bar Blues in the Key of G

PART 2: BLUES STYLES

By now, you have read a lot about the important musical ideas and music theory you need to play the blues. The second part of this book is dedicated to understanding blues styles. Before these styles are explained, it's important to ask the question, "What is the blues?" There are a few ways to answer this question. As we have already learned, the blues is a specific form. It is also a way to approach melodies with blue notes. Fundamentally, however, the blues is the name of a music genre that developed in the deep South and later spread to the major industrial cities of the United States. As the musical ideas of the blues spread, regional and individual blues styles developed. Part 2 of this book traces those developments and explains how to play the many and varied styles that blues musicians have innovated and influenced.

Chapter 5: Early Blues

Blues Origins and History

The story of the blues began long before 1900, when the first blues songs were heard. For centuries, West Africans were taken from their homes and enslaved in America to provide labor. Most of these African men and women were brought to work on the vast plantations of the American South. Although these Africans could not bring their musical instruments with them, they did bring their musical traditions, particularly, exciting polyrhythms, call and response patterns, non-European tonalities, and a history of storytelling through song.

As American slaves, these Africans were forced to learn English and adopt American cultural and religious practices. Slave owners were also fearful of the Africans' ability to communicate with drums, so the use of drums was banned. After generations of slavery, the African traditions blended with that of the American slave-owners. The slaves developed hybrid approaches to speaking, cooking, worshipping, visual art, dancing, and making music. This combination of African and American cultures gave way to an African-American culture complete with blended musical styles.

Early examples of this new African-American musical style were shouts, chants, field hollers, work songs, and spirituals. These early styles were both expressive and communicative. They were sung and accompanied only by hand claps and work noise. They also incorporated English lyrics and African tinged melodies. These early musical styles had strongly syncopated rhythms and used call and response forms. They often expressed a range of emotions, including despair, hope of escape, religious belief, and work motivation. Like traditional West African music, these new forms had a strong element of improvisation. They were also learned and performed "by ear" without the aid of written music.

Late in the 19th century, a new style of music began to emerge in the South. It was a combination of the African-American musical elements with the use of European instruments, particularly the guitar. Since this new style of folk music was played during non-religious leisure time, it is likely that its development coincided with the emancipation of all slaves following the Civil War. Although technically free, most former slaves remained poor and continued to be subjected to discrimination and racism.

By around 1900, this new folk style was becoming known as the blues, particularly as it changed from ensemble music to a more individual style of expression. Early blues performers were often singers and guitar players with a personalized style. Since many musicians in several locations developed the blues, few specific elements of the style existed in the early days. However, general ideas—such as the use of call and response lyrical patterns, blue notes, and primary chords—were widespread.

Blues on the Move

Although the earliest blues developed in the Mississippi Delta region, professional blues performers—as well as great waves of migration—brought the blues to Memphis, New Orleans, Chicago, and other regions of the country. In each of these regions, new styles developed. (See map below.)

Folk Blues/Delta Blues

The region that gave birth to the blues is the Mississippi Delta. This is the large flood plain on the bank of the Mississippi River south of Memphis and north of New Orleans. Around 1900, it was an area of traditional agriculture, intense poverty, and deep African-American roots. In this hot environment full of racial oppression and poverty, blues musicians sang of people's experiences and emotions at local bars called *juke joints*. The style developments of the Delta region were reflected in other communities of the South. In the early decades of the 20th century, nearly every city and state was developing its own regional blues style, including Texas blues, Memphis blues, East Coast blues, and others.

Scoops and Slides

Two of the most important ways to express blue notes in the Delta blues were through *scoops* and *slides*. Most Delta blues music was played on the guitar and sung. Often, guitarists used glass bottle necks to move around the fretboard, sliding from note to note in smooth, continuous transitions. We can imitate these sounds on the piano by sliding from a black key to a white key with one finger. To do this, you play the black key and then let the same finger slide up (the "scoop") or down (the "slide") to the next key. This is notated using a *grace note,* which is a small note ♪ preceding a main note and has no real rhythmic value of its own.

If the scoop or slide starts with a white key, two fingers are needed and the notes are played in one quick motion to give the same feeling as the slide, but without actually sliding off the key.

To slide using three notes, you must combine the two-finger slide with the one finger slide.

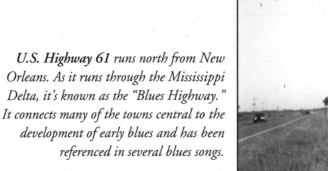

U.S. Highway 61 runs north from New Orleans. As it runs through the Mississippi Delta, it's known as the "Blues Highway." It connects many of the towns central to the development of early blues and has been referenced in several blues songs.

Robert Johnson's Style

By the 1920s, Delta Blues artists had solidified their style. The great bluesmen of this period were Son House, Charley Patton, and Robert Johnson. These early bluesmen were the first to be recorded playing the blues. Robert Johnson (1911–1938), in particular, influenced the generations of musicians that followed him. Johnson spent his relatively short adult life playing blues on street corners and in juke joints. He played quite often in the area around Clarksdale, Mississippi, but traveled up the Mississippi River to Memphis, St. Louis, Chicago, and Detroit. His influential recordings inspired later generations of musicians (including Muddy Waters, Eric Clapton, and many others) to cover his songs. He may be most known for the legend that he sold his soul to the devil to become the king of the Delta bluesmen.

"Clarksdale Blues" is a simple blues in the key of C that mimics the guitar style of Robert Johnson. Although the delta blues was played most often on guitar, the elements of its style influenced the piano blues that would follow it. "Clarksdale Blues" features one of Robert Johnson's classic introductions: a left-hand guitar-like pattern with slides in the right hand.

Track 11 *Clarksdale Blues*

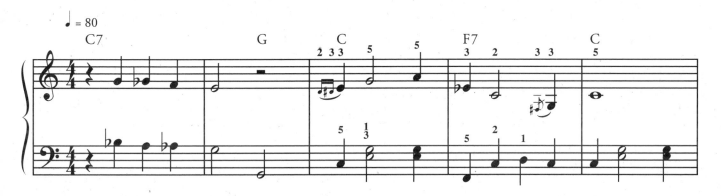

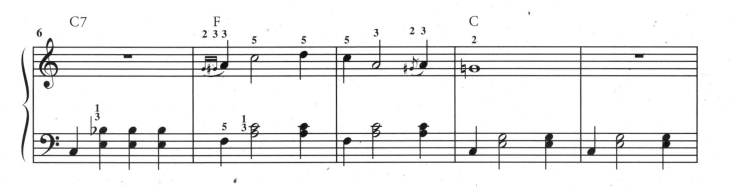

Chapter 6: The Barrelhouse Style

Barrelhouse Blues Piano Style

The earliest style of blues for piano was known as the *barrelhouse* style. In the early 1900s, shacks, sometimes constructed from beer barrels, were hot-spots in African-American communities for socializing and entertainment—particularly in East Texas, Louisiana, and Mississippi. Often, these bars had pianos inside, and blues musicians used these pianos to adapt the blues style to the instrument. Since they weren't classically trained pianists, they developed a unique style of accompaniment to perform the chords of the blues progression.

Flat Four

The basic barrelhouse left-hand pattern contains the root and 5th of the chord played on every beat. This is called the *flat four* because of the four attacks per measure.

The flat four has a number of variations, for example: alternating 5ths and 6ths (Example 12), a pattern of 5th–6th–minor 7th–6th (Example 13), and 5th–5th–6th–5th (Example 14).

"Texarkana Stomp" is a straightforward barrelhouse blues in the key of G. It features a flat four in the left hand and a melody based on the blues scale. Watch out for the ledger lines in both hands. Count down from the lowest note you know to find the right pitch.

Track 16 — *Texarkana Stomp*

A *fermata* indicates that a note should be held longer than its normal duration.

Triplets and the Shuffle Feel

Another important aspect of blues playing is the use of *triplets* and the triplet-based *shuffle*, or *swing*, feel. We have already seen that quarter notes can be divided into two eighth notes. Quarter notes can also be divided into to three even parts. We call these triplets. Eighth-note triplets are written as three eighth notes beamed together with a "3" above or below to indicate the triple division of the beat. When triplets are played in the blues, the first note of the group receives an *accent*. The accent symbol > means to play that note louder than the notes surrounding it. Triplets are counted: 1-&-ah, 2-&-ah, 3-&-ah, 4-&-ah.

15 **Track 17**

Count: 1 & ah 2 & ah 3 & ah 4 & ah

A shuffle feel is based on this triplet subdivision of the beat. When reading a shuffle, the eighth notes are to be treated as if they were the first and third eighths of a triplet. This rhythm is also called *swing eighths* and is used in many styles of music influenced by the blues, including jazz, rock, and rhythm and blues. If a piece is to be played using this swing rhythm, the symbol *Swing 8ths* will appear at the beginning of the music.

Shuffle Rhythm (Swing Eighths)

Written as:

16 **Track 18**

Swing 8ths

Sounds like:

Count: 1 & ah 2 & ah 3 & ah 4 & ah

Barrelhouse Variations

There are a number of variations to the barrelhouse left hand, including the use of straight eighths and swing eighths. Practice each of the following examples until you can play them effortlessly, then try transposing them to different keys.

A

B

C

D *Straight 8ths*

E *Straight 8ths*

F *Swing 8ths*

G *Swing 8ths*

"Rustic Shack Blues" features swing eighths and triplets over a barrelhouse left-hand groove. It is a 12-bar blues in the key of F. Practice the left hand first, and then add the right hand. Remember to accent the first triplet of each group. Watch out for ledger lines, and remember that C♭ is another name for the note B.

 ## Rustic Shack Blues

Note: Play 1st ending, then go back to the beginning and repeat. The 2nd time through the piece, skip over the 1st ending to the 2nd ending, and play to the end.

"Champion" Jack Dupree

"Champion" Jack Dupree (c.1908–1992) was a Louisiana-based blues pianist who epitomized the barrelhouse style. Dupree was a self-taught pianist who grew up an orphan. As a young man, he began playing piano at various drinking establishments. He was also a lightweight boxer, which helped him earn his colorful nickname. Dupree's piano playing brought him to Chicago and, eventually, Europe. His style was defined by *tremolos* and other right-hand flourishes, while his left hand played a raucous and driving barrelhouse groove.

Tremolos

Right-hand tremolos are a major part of Dupree's barrelhouse style. A tremolo is similar to a *trill*, which is a rapid alternation between two adjacent notes. Trills are sometimes notated in their entirety, but mostly, they are indicated with a *tr* above the notes.

In a tremolo, these rapidly alternating notes are played at a larger interval. In the blues, tremolos between notes a 4th, 6th, and octave apart are common. Like trills, tremolos can be written out completely, or indicated by three thick black lines between the notes.

Blues pianists also perform entire chords as tremolos by breaking the three or more notes of a chord into two parts and alternating them rapidly. The most common way to do this is to split the higher notes of the chord off from the bottom note (played with the thumb) and quickly alternate the thumb with the rest of the hand. The thumb provides an excellent counter-weight to the rest of the hand, and this results in balanced, shimmering chords.

"Champion's Blues" reflects the piano style of Jack Dupree, which is epitomized by right-hand tremolos and a swinging left-hand groove. Notice the extra F7 chord in measure 7.

That's a typical Dupree substitution. In this song, playing both hands together presents a challenge, so practice them separately, and put them together slowly.

Track 24 *Champion's Blues*

Swing 8ths ♩ = 100

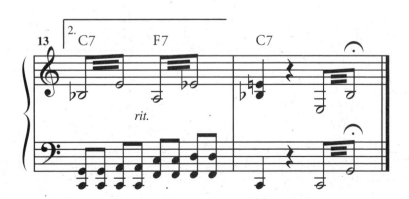

Classic Intros, Endings, and Turnarounds

In all blues styles, there are stock introductions, endings, and *turnarounds*. A turnaround is a short interlude that concludes one chorus before you go on to the next. As you play the exercises in this book and listen to various blues recordings, you will hear these phrases over and over again, often with subtle variations. Many of them are interchangeable. Each example below includes an intro/turnaround version (which can be used to start the piece or lead back to the top of the form) and an ending version (which brings a song to a close). Try playing them with both swing and straight eighths.

Two-Handed Variations

While all of the examples from the previous page can be played with both hands by doubling at the octave or adding chords, there are a few other ways for both hands to play intros, turnarounds, and endings. Check out the examples below.

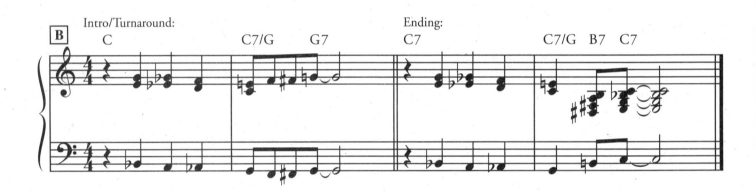

Introduction to Blues Improvisation

Improvisation, which can be defined as "making up music on the spot," is a large component of the blues style, just as it is in jazz, funk, and other American music genres. Often in a blues song, while verses are sung or played, there is room for a piano *fill* in the space between phrases. A fill is a short, improvised idea. Typically, these fills are based on the same blues ideas as the song's melody. Fills help to initiate a layer of call and response between the melody and the improvising instrument. Blues scales, tremolos, and syncopated right-hand chords (like Example 39, page 76) are often used for improvisation. One of the most important aspects of improvising is playing a rhythm that works with the groove of the tune. Try playing some of the same rhythms you hear in the other blues songs and you will be on the right track. Look at the lead sheet version of "Clarksdale Blues" below. Play along with the recording, and practice improvising fills between the phrases of the melody.

Clarksdale Blues

Track 27

Learning to improvise is like learning a new language. In fact, conversing in language is a type of improvisation. In order to be successful, you need to listen to others speaking to learn the vocabulary and how to put the phrases together. The same is true of musical improvisation. This book, as well the blues recordings you listen to, will help provide both the vocabulary and ideas about how to use it in musical phrases. If you want to be a good improviser, try your best to absorb as much vocabulary as possible from recordings and performances. Then, like an inventive author, try to put the vocabulary together into creative musical phrases.

Chapter 7: New Orleans Blues

New Orleans and the Caribbean Influence

At the southern end of the Mississippi River is the city of New Orleans. In the late 1800s and early 1900s, it was not only a bustling port city for trade in the Gulf of Mexico and the Caribbean Sea, but also a melting pot with a large African-American and multi-ethnic population (including people who traced their lineage back to Spain and France). It even had a large population of free African-Americans before the Civil War. As a melting pot of American, African, Caribbean, and European cultures, New Orleans developed its own traditions that were quite different from anywhere else in the United States. At the start of the 20th century, diverse musical elements—including military parade music, ragtime, African, and Latin music—melded together to form jazz. At the same time, New Orleans was developing its own style of blues that was often piano driven. Since New Orleans music is always intensely rhythmic, its blues style is often referred to as New Orleans rhythm and blues.

Straight Eighths Feel

New Orleans blues has a strong Caribbean influence in its rhythm. This includes the use of straight eighth notes. Unlike swing eighths, these are played exactly as written. New Orleans pianists managed to combine straight eighths with a laid-back feel to create a blues style that reflected the free and easy party atmosphere of New Orlean's famous Bourbon Street and Mardi Gras celebration.

The Clave

The early jazz pianist and composer Jelly Roll Morton said, "Jazz has always had a Spanish tinge." He was referring to the musical ties that New Orleans jazz and blues had to the Spanish Caribbean. In fact, New Orleans's music borrows rhythms from the Cuban *clave*. The clave (pronounced CLAH-veh) is an element of Cuban music that comes directly from West African music. It is a rhythmic foundation on which all of the interlocking grooves and polyrhythms are based. Though there are many types of claves, New Orleans music borrowed mostly from the one known as *son clave*, a two-part rhythm with three hits on one side and two on the other. Some grooves make exact use of the son clave, while others use the three-hit side (or just "three side") repeatedly, like the bass line at the top of the next page.

There are two son clave rhythms: one where the two side is played first (known as the 2-3 son clave) and one where the three side is played first (known as the 3-2 son clave). New Orleans music predominantly used the 3-2 son clave. Check out the two rhythms below.

A Son Clave 2-3   B Son Clave 3-2

Check out the following New Orleans blues bass line. Rhythmically, it is the three side of the clave.

8- and 16-Bar Blues Progressions

Another element of New Orleans rhythm and blues—and other early blues styles—was the use of chord progressions that were not 12 bars long. Sometimes, the early folk blues musicians simply added a few bars here and there to accompany awkward vocal phrases, or as extra material at the end of a chorus. Sometimes, these early blues songs ended up with a few choruses of 14 bars. As the blues style developed, the 12-bar form became standard. In New Orleans, where the 8- and 16-bar phrases of marches and ragtime music had more influence, you can find some very well thought out blues forms containing 8 or 16 bars. Following are some possible progressions for 8- and 16-bar blues. Each of the examples is written in the key of C and includes Roman numerals for the chords.

8-Bar Blues—Version 1

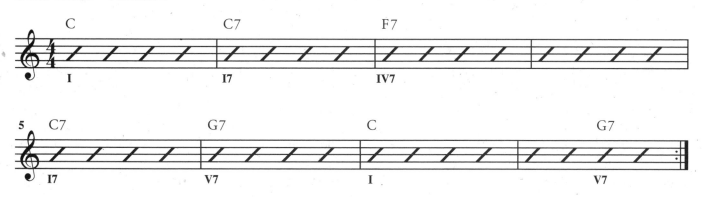

8-Bar Blues—Version 2

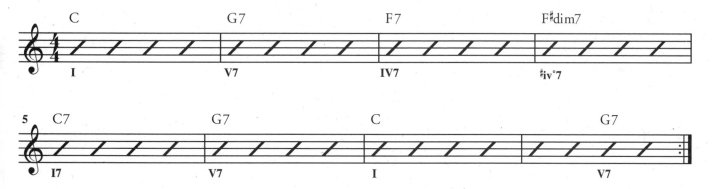

16-Bar Blues—Version 1

C7

I7

5

9   F7   C7

IV7   I7

13   G7   F7   C

V7   IV7   I

16-Bar Blues—Version 2

C7

I7

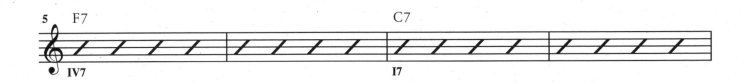

5   F7   C7

IV7   I7

9   G7   F7   G7   F7

V7   IV7   V7   IV7

13   G7   F7   C

V7   IV7   I

Professor Longhair's "Rhumba Boogie" Style

Professor Longhair (1918–1980) enjoyed a long career as a New Orleans blues pianist, singer, and performer. His real name was Roy Byrd, but because of his great skill, he was nicknamed a "piano professor" by a club owner. This, combined with his long hair, resulted in his descriptive nickname. He was a tremendous influence on later New Orleans pianists like Fats Domino and Dr. John. As well as playing barrelhouse and other blues styles, he brought a clave-based Caribbean feel to blues and early rhythm and blues piano. This style is often called *rhumba boogie* because it combined American elements (boogie) with the Latin feel (rhumba). The basic groove for piano is as follows.

Broken Chords

Another element of Professor Longhair's style featured broken chords called *arpeggios*. "Arpeggio" is an Italian word that refers to playing the notes of a chord one at a time rather than simultaneously. New Orleans pianists played these arpeggios in a syncopated way, reflecting the way chords are played in Cuban music. Syncopation occurs when emphasis is shifted from the *onbeats* (1, 2, 3, 4) to the *offbeats,* or &s ("ands"), of the beats. Check out the syncopated arpeggio example below.

New Orleans Piano Licks

New Orleans pianists have developed a wealth of piano ideas that every blues pianist should know. The most important of these is the New Orleans turnaround and its variations.

Ornamented Eighth-Note Line Featuring 6ths

Triplet Arpeggios with a Chromatic Opening

Tremolo Octaves

The Classic New Orleans Turnaround

Take a good look at the turnaround written above. It contains a *sixteenth-note triplet,* which is three notes in the space of half of a beat. This is a rhythm you will hear often in New Orleans music, so listen to the recorded example and try to play along.

"The Professor's Blues" puts these ideas together in an 8-bar blues in F. Practice the licks separately, and then try playing them with a steady left hand. Try inventing your own fills in the New Orleans style.

Track 36 · The Professor's Blues

Chapter 8: Chicago Blues

Introduction to Chicago Blues

During the first part of the 20th century, millions of African-Americans migrated from the deep South to industrial cities in the Northeast and Midwest to seek opportunity and escape racism. Many blues musicians also travelled up the Mississippi River to Chicago and Detroit. By the 1940s, a large African-American community was established in Chicago and the city was developing its own blues style. The Chicago blues was a transformation of the folk and Delta styles of the South.

Muddy Waters, the most notable of the Chicago bluesmen, revolutionized the blues by featuring electric guitar, electric bass, drumset, and piano in his band. Eventually, the use of electric instruments became synonymous with the idea of an urbanized blues sound. The Chicago blues scene produced numerous talented and innovative blues musicians, including Howlin' Wolf, Willie Dixon, Elmore James, and many others. A number of blues record companies also developed in Chicago at this time. The most famous of these is Chess Records. Clubs specifically dedicated to featuring blues performers also sprang up, particularly on the city's South Side.

The Piano in Chicago Blues

As Chicago blues bands grew larger and more amplified, the "sound" of the piano changed so that it could be heard among the electric guitars, bass, drums, harmonica, and, sometimes, even horn sections. Cutting intervals such as octaves and 4ths were played in a high range in order to be heard over the band. Chicago blues pianists like Otis Spann, Earl Boyd, and Roosevelt Sykes also experimented with more complex chords such as *9th chords*.

9th Chords

9th chords add another 3rd on top of 7th chords, resulting in a chord that includes the interval of a 9th above the root. A 9th is the distance of an octave plus one step. The *dominant 9th* chord can be constructed with a major 3rd, perfect 5th, minor 7th, and major 9th. Its formula is: 1–3–5–♭7–9. In other words, it's like a dominant 7th chord with an added 9th. This is a great to chord to use at the end of a Chicago blues song.

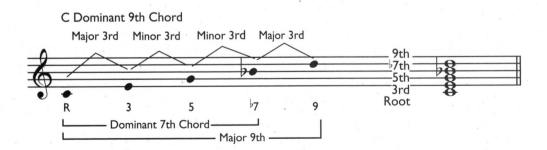

Chicago Shuffle Feel

An important aspect of Chicago-style blues is the use of triplets and the triplet-based shuffle feel. In the chapter on barrelhouse playing (page 54), you learned how these are played. Keep in mind when reading a shuffle that you are to treat the eighth notes as if they were written as the first and third notes of an eighth-note triplet. See below.

Written as:

Played like:

Chicago Bass Patterns

Chicago-style bass players and pianists developed a variety of bass lines to fit with drummers' shuffle feels. These shuffle bass lines were very different and more colorful than the barrelhouse left-hand ideas that preceded them. They involved outlining the notes of the chord in various configurations, like below.

Extended Intro

Chicago blues musicians also innovated an extended intro that has become common in blues performance. It's four measures long and includes one measure of the V7 chord, a measure of the IV chord, then one of the classic turnarounds.

Stop Time

One of the most interesting innovations of the Chicago blues musicians was the idea of *stop time*. Stop time is a series of ensemble hits at the most important points in the blues form. On each chord change, the entire band plays an accented note and then rests until the next chord is played. In this space, a soloist can improvise, or a vocalist can sing. It's a great way to break up the many choruses of a blues song. Sometimes blues bandleaders will call for stop time unexpectedly in performance by using hand gestures to cue the band. Other songs have stop time sections composed into their form.

Stop Time Hits for a Blues in the Key of D

Ornamented Stop Time

Otis Spann's Chicago Style

Otis Spann (1930–1970) was the pianist in Muddy Waters' band during the 1950s and 1960s. Spann was born in Jackson, Mississippi, but like so many others, he moved to Chicago in the 1940s. The Chicago pianist Big Maceo Merriweather took the young Spann under his wing. Soon, he was playing driving piano on all of the Muddy Waters hits. He also made some notable records as a leader. His style was characterized by fast blues scale runs, tremolos, and triplet chords played in the upper register. Below are some examples of his style. Notice the *cluster chords* in Example C. These are chords that include adjacent scale tones and/or chromatic notes.

Tremolo from 5 to ♭7

Treble Chords Played with 4ths

Cluster Chords with Both the 5 and ♭5

Repetitive Scoops

"South Side Blues" is in the style of Otis Spann and includes some of his classic licks and a Chicago shuffle bass line in the key of D. Treble measures 19–20, 23–24, 31–32, and 37–38 are left empty so you can practice improvising fills.

South Side Blues

Ottava alta (abbrev. 8va) tells you to play the notes
one octave higher than written.

Chapter 9: Boogie Woogie

Introduction to Boogie Woogie

During the 1920s, a piano-driven style of blues developed throughout the South and Midwest. As the barrelhouse pianists followed the migration to the cities along the Mississippi River, the piano styles of the blues became more urban and sophisticated. These changes culminated in the style called *boogie woogie*. Boogie woogie's major characteristic is a powerful left-hand bass pattern that usually includes rhythms played on every eighth-note at a fast tempo. This is sometimes called *eight to the bar* (because of the eight eighth notes played per measure). The repetitious left-hand pattern outlines the harmony of the 12-bar blues progression, while the right hand colors the driving left hand with chords and improvisatory lines. The basic left-hand pattern may present little difficulty to the intermediate pianist, but the advanced version doubles every bass note with rolling octaves and can be quite challenging to play.

Boogie woogie pianists could sing and play for dancers as a one-man band, or they could be joined by a full ensemble. In 1928, Clarence "Pine Top" Smith made the boogie woogie style famous with the release of his recording "Pine Top's Boogie Woogie." His music influenced all of the other major boogie woogie pianists, including Jimmy Yancey, Albert Ammons, Meade "Lux" Lewis, Pete Johnson, Charles "Cow Cow" Davenport, and Cripple Clarence Lofton. These pianists helped to develop the boogie style in its heyday from 1925–1945. By the 1950s, boogie woogie's popularity waned as the Chicago blues bands began to electrify the blues. Boogie woogie had a lasting impact through its influence on early rock and roll.

The earliest version of a boogie bass line was a syncopated, swinging eight-to-the-bar version of the barrelhouse flat four (page 52). Try playing the left-hand style below. Boogie woogie, like most blues, is played without using the sustain pedal because it tends to blur all the notes together. Practice it with a light touch, but make sure every note can be heard. Take care to balance each chord.

The Jimmy Yancey Style

While many of the early boogie woogie pianists played the syncopated variation of the barrelhouse left hand as seen above, Jimmy Yancey (1898–1951) and the other Chicago pianists preferred to play a variety of single-note left-hand lines. This freed up the bass line and lightened the overall feel of the style. Often, Yancey would play several of these bass lines in the same song. Yancey's signature move was to conclude each song with a tag ending in the key of E♭, no matter what the key.

Basic Boogie Woogie Bass Lines

You will notice as you play the following lines that some of them resemble the Chicago and New Orleans styles you have already learned. That's because blues musicians borrowed ideas from whatever interested them, especially as travel around United States became easier and recordings more accessible. Borrowing from other styles helped to create a wide variety of blues music with many similar ideas to pull the body of work together. Below are some basic boogie woogie bass lines.

Advanced Boogie Technique

The pianists that were influenced by Jimmy Yancey expanded his style into a raucous, driving groove that required advanced piano technique. The most impressive of these new skills was to double all of the left-hand boogie woogie bass notes at the octave and continuously alternate between the two octaves to create a bouncing eight to the bar. See example below.

Right-Hand Ideas

Boogie woogie pianists employed a number of lightly articulated, "sprinkley" right-hand lines and interludes using the blues scale, slides, and chords. Following are some examples of this.

Syncopated Right-Hand Chords

Bugle-Like Single Lines (Reminiscent of Military Bugle Calls)

Triplet-Based Combinations of the Single Lines and Chords

Albert Ammons, Meade "Lux" Lewis, and Pete Johnson

By the 1930s, boogie woogie was experiencing a wave of popularity, and three pianists stood out as the masters of the genre. They had gained so much notoriety that they were invited to perform at Carnegie Hall in New York, which in turn set off a boogie woogie craze. All three pianists achieved a virtuosic level of technique and were engagingly musical players.

Albert Ammons (1907–1949) was arguably the most powerful of the three. Born and raised in Chicago, he played in Chicago clubs starting in the 1920s. He led his own band and made a number of recordings. Ammons played continuously through the 1940s, gaining fame and ultimately performing at President Truman's inauguration in 1949, shortly before he died. Of all of the boogie woogie left-hand patterns, he preferred to play the one below.

Meade "Lux" Lewis (1905–1964) was also from Chicago and played regularly in the clubs at the same time as Albert Ammons. He is most known for his song "Honky Tonk Train Blues" (1927), which was recorded a number of times by various musicians. Lewis was also interested in non-piano keyboard instruments and was recorded playing harpsichord and celeste in the 1940s. Lewis was perhaps the most complex of the three. His style was characterized by inventive development of musical ideas. He often based each chorus of a song on one technical idea, using at times stride and walking bass lines. In this way, he was able sustain songs for 20–30 minutes at times.

Pete Johnson (1904–1967) was born in Kansas City, Missouri and began his career as a drummer, but switched to piano in the early 1920s. He played in Kansas City throughout the 1920s and 1930s and moved to Buffalo, New York in the 1950s. More so than the other two pianists, he was sought after to play in bands and accompany singers. He often performed with singers like Big Joe Turner and Jimmy Rushing.

Jump Blues

By the 1940s, elements of big band jazz, blues, and boogie woogie merged to form a popular style known as *jump blues*. This was an uptempo style played by a small band featuring a small horn section and vocalists. At its heart was the boogie woogie style bass line played by piano and accompanied by drums, rhythm guitar, and acoustic bass. It also featured a small horn section with shouting vocals and honking saxophones often trading call-and-response ideas. By playing jump blues, musicians such as Tiny Bradshaw and Johnny Otis kept the boogie woogie style alive well into the 1950s, when it became one of the major influences of early rock and roll.

"Evolution Boogie" is a boogie woogie tune that works through several of the boogie bass lines and right-hand ideas starting with a Jimmy Yancey-oriented feel and ending with challenging bouncing octaves. It can be played anywhere from 125–175 beats per minute. Try playing it slowly at first and then at faster tempos. You could also experiment with adding your own solo ideas. For more about soloing, see page 80.

Evolution Boogie

Track 48

More About Improvisation

Improvising Solos

You have already learned how to improvise fills in a blues verse. After a few verses are sung, it's time for a piano, guitar, or harmonica solo. In instrumental blues songs, after the melody is played, instruments can perform solos. This doesn't actually mean they play all by themselves. It means they are the featured improviser for a few choruses, while the other instruments hold down the basic groove. Taking a blues solo means inventing your own melody over the chord changes. It's important that you keep track of where you are in the form so you can finish at the end of a chorus and not in the middle. Try using the blues scale, tremolos, slides, syncopated right-hand chords, and any other blues ideas you've learned to create an interesting solo. Look through the songs in this book. They are full of ideas for soloing. It's also important to listen to other blues pianists like Otis Spann, Albert Ammons, and Meade "Lux" Lewis to hear what their solos sound like. This will help you develop your own ideas. Try to play along with the following Chicago style blues.

Track 49 — Chicago Blues Play-Along

Chapter 10: Stride and Ragtime

Scott Joplin and Ragtime

Although not a style of blues, both ragtime and the blues were influenced by the same early styles of African-American music. Ragtime, however, also draws inspiration from European classical music and military marches. It is essentially a cosmopolitan piano style, which, unlike early jazz and blues was completely notated. Ragtime developed at the same time as the blues, and both styles had great influence on American popular music. Since it developed in the late 1800s and early 1900s, its growth predated the use of recording technology. It was, however, widely disseminated through sheet music and piano rolls for player pianos.

The essence of ragtime was the idea of a "rag" or syncopated march that combined an *oom-pah* left hand (alternating between the root and 5th of the chord on the first and third beats of the measure) with exciting rhythmic melodies in the right hand. The syncopations were sometimes called "ragged," and the name "ragtime" came into use as an expression of this syncopated style of playing. Although rhythmically influenced by African-American music, ragtime forms were borrowed from classical music. They utilized 8-bar phrases and multiple themes.

Scott Joplin (1867–1917), known as the "King of Ragtime," was ragtime's foremost composer. He wrote 44 rags, a ballet, and two operas. Although born in Eastern Texas, he travelled throughout the South and Mississippi River valley, studying music, performing, and composing. It was during this time that he wrote his most famous compositions, "Maple Leaf Rag" and "The Entertainer." In 1907, he moved to New York with the hope of finding a producer for his opera *Treemonisha*. He died in New York 10 years later.

Scott Joplin and ragtime had a tremendous influence on the styles of popular American music that followed it. In New York, ragtime gave way to the *stride* pianists (see page 82), while in New Orleans, it greatly influenced Jelly Roll Morton and the earliest jazz musicians. Ragtime was also a major influence on the Piedmont blues style of the East Coast (see next page).

The Piedmont Blues

While the other regional styles were developing, the Southeast coast stretching from Richmond, Virginia to Atlanta, Georgia was developing its own blues style influenced by ragtime, country dance tunes, and fingerstyle guitar playing. Piedmont blues doesn't refer to one particular style but a variety of styles within the Southeast region mostly played by guitar players such as Blind Blake, Blind Willie McTell, and Barbeque Bob. The primary element of Piedmont blues is a fingerpicking guitar style where the bass notes alternate with syncopated treble notes to provide an accompaniment style similar to ragtime but performed on the guitar.

The Left-Hand Stride Style

At the same time the boogie woogie style was developing in the Midwest, pianists in Harlem, New York were creating a new style known as stride piano. By the 1920s, pianists in New York City, including James P. Johnson and Lucky Roberts, were inventing a style of piano playing based on combining ragtime with the blues. In this new style, the pianist's left hand would stride across the bottom half of the piano, spanning great distances between bass notes and chords. The main idea of stride is that on beats 1 and 3 of a measure of $\frac{4}{4}$, the left hand plays a single bass note, or a bass note with an added octave, 5th, or other interval, while on beats 2 and 4, the left hand plays a chord farther up the piano. This creates an oom-pah effect that provides a groove for the entire piece of music and allows for melodies, accompaniments, or improvisations to be performed with the right hand. Check out the example below.

The essential stride groove can be broken up by interjections of walking 10ths, as seen below (also, see measures 4, 8, 11, and 12 of "125th Street Blues" on the next page). This yields some variety and interest to the left-hand pattern and works well when transitioning to a IV or V chord, or during a turnaround. Not every pianist can play these wide intervals, so you may need to *roll* the 10ths (play the two notes in quick succession), or play octaves instead.

There were many excellent stride players on the East Coast who often competed in Harlem "cutting contests," or musical challenges, to see who could play the fastest, cleanest, and most creative stride piano. Among the most famous of these were Willie "the Lion" Smith and Fats Waller, a student of James P. Johnson who became known for his compositions "Ain't Misbehavin'" and "Honeysuckle Rose," as well as for his excellent piano playing.

Although influenced by the blues, stride was truly a style of early jazz. Its chord progressions and phrases are more influenced by ragtime, but it contained the improvisatory and aggressive nature of the blues. Starting in the 1930s, the jazz pianist Art Tatum took stride playing to a new extreme of speed and technique.

"125th Street Blues" is a Harlem stride-style blues in the key of B♭. It uses both the oom-pah and walking 10ths patterns. If you can't reach a 10th, use your right hand to play the upper notes in measures 4, 8, 11, and 12. Be sure to play the left hand quietly enough so that it doesn't overpower the right-hand melody. If you take care to perform the *staccato* and accent marks, you will achieve an authentic stride feel. Staccato means short, detached. Play these notes—the ones with a dot above or below the notehead—in a short, detached way.

125th Street Blues

Track 52

Chapter 11: Gospel Blues

Gospel and the Blues

Just as blues musicians incorporated ragtime into the blues to form new styles, they also borrowed from jazz, gospel, and other popular music styles. Like ragtime, gospel's growth runs parallel to that of the blues, and both genres have much in common. In fact, some musicians claim that if you were to take a blues and substitute the word "God" for "baby," you would have a gospel song. It's not exactly that easy, because gospel has its own rich tradition.

Gospel is a religious musical genre originally derived from early African-American spirituals. It is used both for Christian religious services and for reflection or entertainment. While gospel, like jazz, developed into its own distinct style with varied subgenres extending into the 21st century, it shares many stylistic elements with the blues. Blues artists such as Blind Lemon Jefferson sometimes performed a kind of gospel blues, which melded blues guitar with evangelical lyrics.

Rubato Style

One of the techniques that blues artists borrowed from gospel is playing *rubato*. Rubato (Italian for "robbed") means playing with robbed time, or out of time. This implies playing without meter. For a keyboard player, this allows you to change chords whenever you feel like it, or when your ear tells you. Gospel rubato playing often provides music for transitions between parts of the service, or when someone is offering a prayer or sermon. Rubato playing is also a very useful technique for developing solo piano introductions. Try playing the chords below, holding them for as long as you like. If the spirit moves you, try improvising some solo lines to help connect the chords.

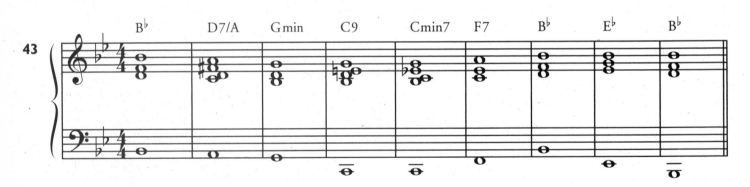

Playing the B-3 Organ

Until now, all of the examples and styles in this book have been played on the piano. In gospel music, a large part of the repertoire is played on the electric organ. While a number of organs were used in gospel churches, the Hammond B-3 eventually became the organ of choice for gospel performances. Since the 1950s, it has been an essential element of much jazz, blues, rock, and gospel music.

B-3 Basics

While you can approximate the sound of a B-3 on many of today's electronic keyboards, it's fun to try playing the real thing. The B-3 has two *manuals* (keyboards) and a pedal board, which allows you to play bass notes with your feet. Using drawbars, Leslie speakers, and a few other effects, you can generate a variety of organ tones.

An organ's drawbars manipulate the different pitches that sound while pressing down one key. They allow a fundamental note to be played with a variety of other notes like the octave below, as well as a number of octaves and perfect 5ths above the original note. Pulling drawbars in and out, or in any combination, can lead to some really great organ sounds. If you can get your hands on a B-3, try some of the different drawbar combinations. There are also some presets you can try. You can access these by pressing down the black keys all the way to the left of the manuals.

B-3 drawbars.

B-3s also come with a percussion effect. When toggled on, this effect produces a "plinking" sound at the start of each tone. This provides each note with a clearer articulation. B-3 players also find ways to exploit the percussiveness of the organs natural key clicking and popping sounds. Probably the most interesting effect comes from special speakers known as Leslies, and not from the organ itself. These speakers are equipped with a rotating baffle that allows for a tremolo, vibrato, and chorus effects. These Leslies can be set for fast or slow rotation.

Interior of a Leslie speaker.

Advanced B-3 Ideas

Many jazz, blues, and gospel organists use a number of advanced organ techniques to achieve an authentic style. Below is a list of ideas to experiment with as you develop your organ technique. Since nearly every aspect of the tone can be manipulated on the instrument, you have the opportunity to develop a very personalized style.

Using the Manuals

Since you can set up different sounds on the two manuals, you can choose to use one for bass tones and one for chords or melodies. Jazz pianists tend to use the bottom one for a bass sound, while blues and gospel players tend to use the bottom manual for chords and melodies. Most blues performers choose not to use the pedals at all.

"Popping" the Keys

Track 53

Try gently tapping a fist full of notes and you will get a popping sound you can use as a percussive effect. Carefully placed pops can add depth to your groove.

Alternating Manuals

Track 54

For another interesting effect, set the drawbars to a different configuration for each manual. Then, alternate between the manuals, playing the same chord back and forth in quick succession.

Repetitive Notes

Track 55

Playing the same note rapidly on the organ creates another percussive effect. Try using the fingering: 3, 2, 1; 3, 2, 1; and so on.

Long Notes

Track 56

There are plenty of ways to add excitement to long notes or held out chords. Try reaching up and adjusting the drawbar settings while holding out a chord, or switching on the different Leslie speeds, and listen to the sound.

Not everyone has access to a real B-3 Hammond organ. If you are playing an electronic keyboard, see if there is a way to adjust the drawbar settings or add a Leslie effect to your sound; often, a tone wheel will allow you to emulate the sound of a Leslie. Try out some of the extended effects to hear how they sound on your keyboard. If you want to hear a master playing the B-3, check out jazz/blues organist Jimmy Smith.

Secondary Dominants

One of gospel's influences on modern blues is the use of colorful advanced harmony featuring *secondary dominant* chords. You will remember from Part 1 (page 35) that the dominant chord is a dominant 7th chord that resolves to the tonic chord (V7 to I). A secondary dominant chord extends this dominant function outside of the initial key and allows for dominant chords, or V chords, to be placed before any of the chords in a song. Take any chord from the key of C, let's say the ii chord, Dmin. What would the

V chord be if we were in the key of D Minor? The answer is A7. We can use that A7 chord to resolve to Dmin, but we can do it while still in the key of C. We call that A7 chord the "V7 of ii" (V7/ii), or a secondary dominant. Basically, you can precede any chord with a dominant 7th chord a 5th above it. Look at the progression below, it shows the secondary dominants for all of the diatonic chords in the key of C Major.

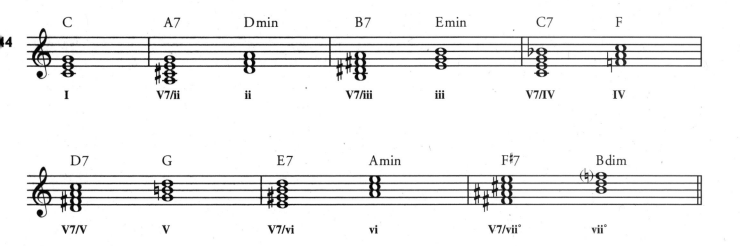

Note that the V7 of vii° is rarely used because the diminished chord doesn't provide a very stable target for the secondary dominant. All of the others appear frequently in many genres of music. Let's look at the secondary dominants for the key of G as well.

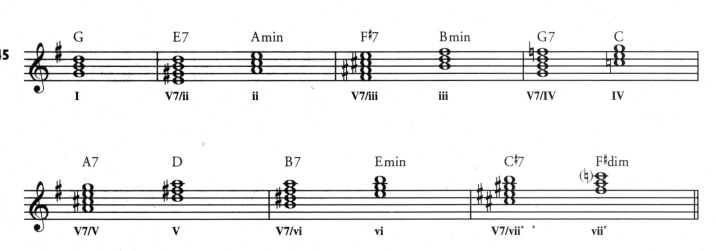

More Secondary Dominants

Secondary dominants can give a piece of music some real harmonic push and pull. Below are a few more harmonic ideas to play around with. Not only can you precede any chord with its V chord, you can precede secondary dominants with their V chords, too; this can lead to a chain of secondary dominants. Another type of secondary dominant can be created using the fully diminished 7th chord. These diminished chords can precede any chord from a half step below. Diminished chords can also fit between any two chords that have stepwise root motion. That type of secondary dominant is called a *passing diminished chord*, and it is very common in gospel chord progressions.

Below is a sample chord progression using a variety of secondary dominants.

Blues in Triple Meter

Blues Progression in $\frac{3}{4}$

One of the most important ways that gospel music influenced the blues is the use of the triple meter. In $\frac{3}{4}$, there are three beats to a measure and the quarter note gets one beat. Here's how a blues progression maps out in $\frac{3}{4}$. Note that in this feel, the eighths are still swung.

Blues Progression in $\frac{6}{8}$

Another metric variation is $\frac{6}{8}$. In this time signature, there are six beats per measure, and the eighth note receives one beat. $\frac{6}{8}$ can also feel like two large beats, each with a triple subdivision (counted: **1**, 2, 3, **4**, 5, 6). A classic $\frac{6}{8}$ gospel feel has a "backbeat," or accent, on beat 4.

Blues Progression in $\frac{12}{8}$

In $\frac{12}{8}$, there are 12 beats in each measure and the eighth note gets one beat. Another way to think of $\frac{12}{8}$ is there are four large beats in each measure and each beat has a triple subdivision (counted: **1**, 2, 3, **4**, 5, 6, **7**, 8, 9, **10**, 11, 12). We've already looked at a shuffle; that's a style that could be written in $\frac{12}{8}$ instead of using triplets or swing eighths. The example below uses the $\frac{12}{8}$ time signature to notate a slow gospel-style blues.

"Sunday Blues" is a slow, bluesy gospel tune in $\frac{3}{4}$ time. While its melody is very bluesy, the tune also contains a variety of secondary dominants and a section for improvising. You could play this song on piano or organ.

Whichever you choose, take a close look at the clefs at the beginning of the piece. Both hands are playing in the bass clef. This provides a dark, sonorous register for the melody and chords.

Track 57 *Sunday Blues*

Chapter 12: Rhythm and Blues to Rock and Roll

Starting in the late 1940s, the term "rhythm and blues" was being used by record companies to describe a range of African-American popular music styles, including the blues itself. The term came to be used to market all kinds of African-American popular music, including jump blues, boogie woogie, Chicago blues, New Orleans blues, and other regional styles. The growth of the recording industry, and the appeal of so-called "race records," led to the founding of several new record labels in the 1940s that were dedicated to putting out rhythm and blues records. These included Atlantic, Specialty, and Imperial.

The popularity of rhythm and blues records led to some artists becoming household names across the country, including Little Richard, Fats Domino, Chuck Berry, and Ray Charles—all of whom were essentially playing the blues. These artists had tremendous appeal across racial divides and became crossover sensations selling millions of records.

A Memphis Sound

By the 1950s, white musicians in the South had become interested in playing rhythm and blues in their own way. Particularly influenced by blues, country, bluegrass, and gospel, they were playing an early form of rock and roll known as *rockabilly*. Memphis, Tennessee—with its long tradition of blues, gospel, and country—became a center for the developing style.

Eventually, the term "rock and roll" would come to describe the new sounds that were nearly the same rhythm and blues but performed by white musicians. The early style was a straight- or swing-eighth boogie woogie feel, with an emphatic backbeat played on the snare drum (backbeat occurs when emphasis is placed on beats 2 and 4 of a measure). Like jump blues, this new style had lyrics about good times and love interests, rather than the traditional blues themes. In Memphis, one record label would give birth to rock and roll's most famous acts.

Sun Records, founded by Sam Phillips, put out records for Memphis musicians like Elvis Presley, Jerry Lee Lewis, and Carl Perkins. Bill Haley, who recorded on the Decca label, was also an important early rock and roll musician. His big hit "Rock Around the Clock" and so many other early rock tunes were simple 12-bar blues compositions with many of the same elements as earlier blues songs. By the late 1950s, the worlds of rhythm and blues, and rock and roll were at times indistinguishable. Since the music was nearly the same, important artists like Little Richard were considered to be playing both rhythm and blues as well as rock and roll.

In the 1960s, the sounds began to change as rock music from Great Britain became increasingly popular in the United States. At the same time, rhythm and blues blossomed into styles such as funk, soul, and Motown. All of these new styles were again rooted in the blues and also came to influence the blues.

Playing Off a Riff

Rock and roll, rhythm and blues, and jump blues players before them infused their blues with *riffs*. A riff is a musical idea that provides the *hook,* or melody of interest, in a song. It's often a simple, yet memorable, musical phrase that can be played repeatedly. A well-composed riff can work over all the chord changes of a blues with minimal alterations. Some musicians built entire songs off simple riffs, these types of songs can be very catchy because the riff provides continuity throughout the whole song. See below for some useful blues riffs.

"Whole Lot of Rockin' Goin' On" is a 12-bar blues in the key of A. It's played with straight eighths at a medium-fast tempo and features a number of 1950s rock and roll riffs played over a barrelhouse left hand, including stop time in measures 13–15. The right hand in the last chorus is left open for you to improvise. Try using some *glissandos* to add excitement; for information about these and the other techniques used in this song, see page **96**.

Whole Lot of Rockin' Goin' On

Quindicesima (abbrev. 15ma) tells you to play the notes two octaves higher than written.

Jerry Lee Lewis, Fats Domino, and Little Richard

There are three pianists that epitomized how early rhythm and blues, and rock and roll were played on the piano.

Fats Domino

Fats Domino (b. 1928), originally from New Orleans, had a number of hits on Imperial Records, including "Blueberry Hill" and "Ain't That a Shame." He was heavily influenced by boogie woogie pianists like Albert Ammons and Little Willie Littlefield. His piano style included chords played with continuous triplets in the right hand voiced near middle C, while the left hand played a straightforward boogie bass line. See below.

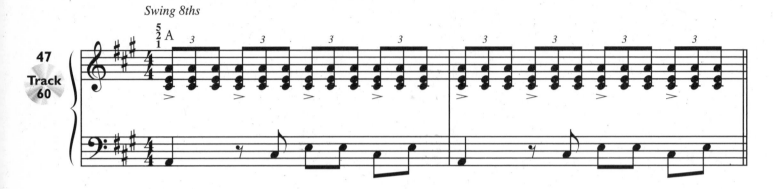

Little Richard

Little Richard (b. 1932) was born Richard Wayne Penniman in Macon, Georgia. His best-selling hits were "Tutti Frutti" and "Good Golly Miss Molly," both of which were swinging 12-bar jump blues complete with honking tenor sax solos. Although Little Richard was probably more well known for his long curly hair, thin moustache, and falsetto cries than for his piano playing, his piano style is a prime example of the rhythm and blues style of the 1950s. His left hand played a straight-eighth version of the classic barrelhouse boogie, while his right hand played continuous eighth note chords. He was prone to playing fills in the upper octave that began with a quick triplet and relaxed back into steady eighth notes. See below.

Jerry Lee Lewis

Jerry Lee Lewis (b. 1935) is probably the most famous of the rock and roll pianists. He was born in Ferriday, Louisiana and grew up playing piano and listening to country, gospel, and blues. In 1956, he moved to Memphis and recorded at Sun Studios. In the late 1950s, he achieved stardom with the hits "Whole Lot of Shakin' Goin' On" and "Great Balls of Fire." He was known as a performer for his onstage antics, such as irreverently kicking the piano bench out from underneath him and playing standing up, while flopping his blond hair in front of his face. As a pianist, he used a number of boogie techniques. He was fond of including pounding eighth notes in 4ths in the highest octave of the piano and using glissandos as fills. A glissando, or gliss, is a slide up or down the white or black keys, briefly touching all of them before ending on a selected note. (The symbol for a gliss is: 〰.) Lewis's glisses are played down from the highest octave to the middle of the keyboard. Sometimes, he played two or three glisses in quick succession, creating great excitement with his fills.

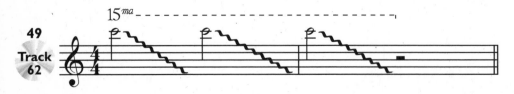

Ray Charles and His Style

Ray Charles (1930–2004) was one of the most well-known rhythm and blues musicians of the 1950s. Although born in Georgia, he grew up mostly in northern Florida. At a young age, he lost his sight. As a child, he learned to play boogie woogie on the piano, as well as classical music and the blues. By the mid-1950s, Charles was recording for Atlantic Records. He had a number of hits with Atlantic, including "Hallelujah I Love Her So" and "What'd I Say." In 1960, he struck a deal with ABC Records that allowed him more artistic control over his recordings. The new contract produced several more hits, such as "Hit the Road Jack," and "I Can't Stop Loving You."

Charles' music was influenced by a number of diverse styles, including rhythm and blues, gospel, jazz, and country. Much of his material incorporates traditional blues elements: the 12-bar blues form, riff-based songs, and call and response (particularly with his backup singers The Raelettes). His keyboard style is somewhat more sparse and relaxed than contemporaries like Jerry Lee Lewis. He often used riff-based patterns and could provide cleverly placed fills. On most songs, he also used syncopated chordal accompaniments as a boogie woogie pianist would. Check out the example below.

He was also well known for his melodic vocal style. Unlike the early blues musicians, he had tremendous vocal flexibility and could sing in both the smooth style of the crooners but also produce grittier blues vocalizations. By infusing his rhythm and blues style with authentic gospel and blues sounds, Ray Charles is often credited with pioneering the next wave of blues-oriented music called "soul."

"Say What?" is a homage to Ray Charles's keyboard style. It's a 12-bar blues in the key of E, except most of the time the E chord is minor. This adds a very effective ambiguity to the tonality. This piece requires a strong left hand and good hand independence. Watch out for the unusual rhythmic idea in measures 37–40. These eighth notes are in groups of three, but they are not triplets (the three-note groups are bracketed in the music). To get the authentic Ray Charles sound, play this piece on a Wurli. (For more information on Wurlitzers, see page 100.)

Say What?

Track 64

Playing Wurlitzer and Fender Rhodes

By the late 1950s, blues pianists were experimenting with electric pianos, particularly the Wurlitzer and Fender Rhodes. Both instruments make a satisfying pianistic tone, while being portable and easily amplified. Best of all, they are played just like a piano. Most Wurlitzers have a 64-note keyboard. They have a modified piano action, in which hammers strike metal reeds rather than strings. These reeds are amplified using an electrostatic pickup. A sustain pedal can also be attached to sustain notes in the same way an acoustic piano does. Wurlitzers, or "Wurlies" as they have been nicknamed, have a sweet metallic tone when played lightly but can have a harsh overdriven sound when played with full arm weight. Wurlies also have a vibrato knob that allows for the sound to waver or shimmer at a variety of rates similar to a vibraphone. Many popular musicians have used them in their recordings, including blues-oriented artists like Ray Charles, Booker T. & the MG's, Buddy Guy, and others.

Wurlitzer electric piano.

In the mid-1960s, the Wurlie's chief competition became the Fender Rhodes. The Rhodes, as it came to be known, used a piano-like action to strike metal tines. To amplify its sound, it used electromagnetic pickups. A number of different models were introduced over the years that ranged from 32 keys to a full 88 keys. Many great musicians have utilized the warm, glowing sound of the Rhodes, including Stevie Wonder, Chick Corea, and Herbie Hancock.

During this era, there were a number of other electric keyboard instruments being used on recordings and performances, but none were as prominent as the Rhodes or Wurlie. Since neither has been in production for some time, like the B-3 organ, they are considered vintage instruments and can sometimes be hard to find. If you have the opportunity to play one, enjoy it. If not, there are a number of electronic keyboards that do a fine job of approximating the sounds of these classic instruments.

PHOTO BY CASINOKAT

Fender Rhodes electric piano.

Chapter 13: Jazz and the Blues

Intro to Jazz

During their development, jazz and blues weren't always considered such different styles as they are today. In fact, musicians in both styles borrowed extensively from each other. Around 1900, African-American musicians in New Orleans began to combine several musical styles—including ragtime, marches, spirituals, and blues—into what would eventually be known as jazz. The first defined style of jazz to emerge was the "traditional," or Dixieland, style from New Orleans, which featured improvised horn solos and ensemble playing over a ragtime feel in the rhythm section. The original instrumentation included piano, banjo, tuba, trombone, clarinet, and trumpet. In the early days of jazz, Jelly Roll Morton was the preeminent pianist and composer.

By the 1920s, the development of jazz had been shaped by notable musicians like Louis Armstrong and Fletcher Henderson. In the 1930s, the instrumentation had developed to include bass, drums, piano, and entire sections of trumpets, trombones, and saxophones. As these big bands played dance music for live and radio audiences, they were often playing a stylized version of the 12-bar blues.

During the late 1940s, bebop pioneers were again reinventing jazz with *dissonant* (clashing) harmonies, *angular* melodies (melodies that move in wider leaps across often dissonant intervals), and smaller bands. Musicians like Charlie Parker and Dizzy Gillespie also reharmonized the blues to fit their new fast-paced modern style. From the 1950s until today, jazz musicians continue to create offshoots of the bebop style, including cool jazz, hard bop, post bop, free jazz, Latin jazz, and fusion—all of which retained some element of blues influence.

Swing Feel

We looked at the swing feel in earlier styles of blues, now let's take another look at it since it is essential to the jazz style. While two swing eighth notes are written exactly the same as two straight eighths, they sound different. Remember, they are played as if they were the first and last note of a triplet.

Written like: Sounds like:

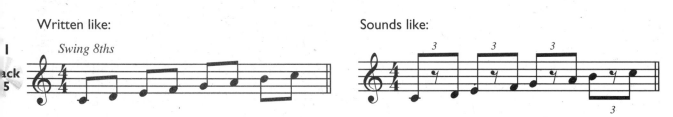

Jazz songs often feature long lines of swing eighths, so it's essential to get the feel right. Compare the two phrases below.

Walking Bass Line

Jazz's major contribution to the blues is the idea of the *walking bass* line. The term "walking" refers to a bass part constructed almost exclusively with quarter notes. These walking quarter notes define the pulse of the song and add to its swinging feel. Walking lines are free to connect chord tones in any way that makes sense. The only rule is to play the root of the chord on the *downbeat* (beat 1) of every measure. Otherwise, you can connect the chords in anyway that sounds good to you. Blues bassists tend to use more chord tones in their bass lines, while jazz players often walk their bass lines using more chromatic notes. Check out the following examples.

Blues Walking Line

Jazz Walking Line

Below is an example of the 12-bar blues played using a walking bass line.

A Kansas City Sound: Count Basie

Kansas City, Missouri is partly known for a style of music that combined elements of blues and jazz into a swinging blues. A number of notable musicians developed their personalized styles in Kansas City, including the boogie woogie pianist Pete Johnson and the jump blues singer Big Joe Turner. Bebopper Charlie Parker also laid his musical foundations playing blues and swing in Kansas City. While the bandleader and pianist Count Basie (1904–1984) was originally from New Jersey, he joined a band that toured Texas and Oklahoma and eventually came to live in Kansas City playing in Bennie Moten's big band.

Starting in the late 1930s, Basie had his own Kansas City big band. A new, swinging feel in the rhythm section was achieved by using a walking bass line, a ride cymbal and hi-hat swing feel on the drumset, the guitarist strumming chords on every beat with accents on 2 and 4, and Basie sporadically interjecting with light treble piano fills. On top, the horns played a series of riffs and accents, which were set up carefully by the drummer. On occasion, Basie also featured blues singers like Jimmy Rushing. While Basie's big band sometimes played fully orchestrated jazz arrangements, they were also known for playing tunes of a completely improvisatory nature, basing them on simple riffs and including jazz solos. These riff-based tunes were essentially a new blues style for big band.

Basie and his band went on to perform countless concerts and released a number of significant records. Eventually moving to New York, they performed across the country and often featured excellent jazz vocalists like Ella Fitzgerald and Sarah Vaughan. The Basie band was one of many jazz big bands that were very popular in the 1930s and 1940s. Although Basie and his band continued to play during the decades after World War II, the popularity of the big bands began to wane and a new jazz style emerged called bebop.

*Justifying his royal nickname, **William "Count" Basie** (1904–1984) became one of the most popular and influential bandleaders in the history of jazz. His sparse, bluesy piano style was similarly notable; Basie played just enough to keep his band swinging.*

"KC's Other Blues" requires you to play the extreme low and high ends of the piano at the same time. It's a 12-bar Basie-style blues with one of his signature endings. It uses a jazzy version of the blues progression (more on this on the next page). Watch out for the *ghost note* in measure 10. A ghost note is played lightly, so that it barely sounds. For an extra challenge, try adding some of your own improvisation.

Track 70 *KC's Other Blues*

Ottava bassa (abbrev. 8vb) tells you to play the notes one octave lower than written.

Bebop Blues

In post-war New York, a new style of jazz was emerging that took its blues origins in a totally new direction. Reflecting the chaotic speed of modern life in the big city, musicians like Charlie Parker, Dizzy Gillespie, and Thelonious Monk began playing a style of jazz with advanced and sometimes dissonant harmonies, as well as intricate and disjointed melodies. This new style came to be called *bebop,* or *rebop,* because these words sounded like the complex syncopations in its rhythms and melodies.

Played primarily by small combos, such as quartets and quintets, bebop was lighter, faster, and more aggressive than the big bands of the previous era. Combos usually included piano, bass, drumset, trumpet, and saxophone. The essential style included a walking bass line and swinging drum beat. Both the drummer and pianist engaged in a rhythmic conversation while accompanying a soloist or melody. Two horns played melodies and solos over the top of this exciting groove.

Although blues elements (especially the 12-bar form) influenced bebop musicians, they greatly altered many of these elements to fit their new style. Bebop players had a deep understanding of harmony, and they set out to reinvent the blues by reharmonizing its chord progression. They did this by using *chord substitutions*; these are new chords, which can be inserted into a progression, that will ultimately bring you to the most important points of the harmonic structure, but in innovative ways. Usually, these chord substitutions take you briefly through keys other than the tonic.

Look at the chord progression below. This is one of the standard ways that beboppers reharmonized the blues. It uses a kind of extended secondary dominant known as a *two-five* (ii–V). Two-fives not only precede a given chord by its V chord, but precede the V chord with a minor ii chord that also belongs to the target key. Jazz musicians use two-fives in a number of different ways, sometimes without resolving them at all. In the progression below, two-fives are used to precede the essential chords of the blues progression. In the last four bars of any jazz blues, a two-five also replaces the original V–IV motion of the early blues.

Bebop Blues Form

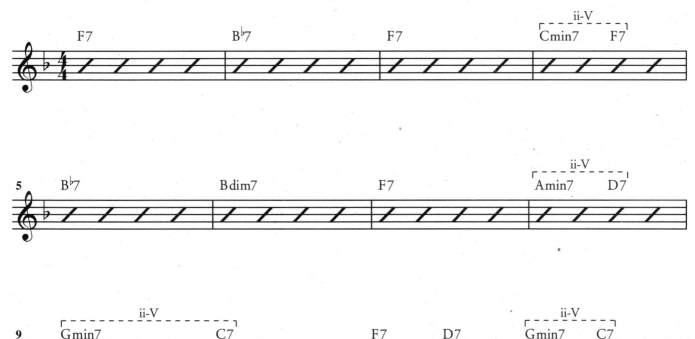

Charlie Parker and the Bird Blues

Charlie Parker (1920–1955) was one of the key innovators of the bebop style. Born in Kansas City, he grew up playing the alto saxophone and learning the Kansas City style of blues and jazz. In the late 1930s, he played swinging blues as a member of Jay McShann's Territory Band. In 1939, he moved to New York and shortly after began jamming with musicians at Milton's Playhouse in Harlem. These jam sessions would eventually spawn the ideas that led to the creation of bebop. Parker's innovative improvisation style included using upper extensions of the chords, such as the 9th, 11th, and 13th, and superimposed chord substitutions. Throughout the 1940s and 1950s, Parker led jazz combos in performance and in the recording of his original material. Unfortunately, the musical genius was also addicted to alcohol and heroin. These addictions led to a deterioration of his body. He developed several serious health issues including ulcers, cirrhosis of the liver, and heart disease. He died at age 34.

Charlie Parker completely reinvented the blues progression into something called the "Bird Blues" after his nickname "Yardbird," or just "Bird." It contains chains of two-fives that move chromatically. Although it moves briefly through several keys, all of the important chords of the blues are left intact. Check out the Bird Blues form below.

Bird Blues Form

Minor Blues and Variations

Both bebop jazz and Chicago blues musicians used a minor key version of the 12-bar blues. There are a few variations, especially in the last four bars of the form. Below, it is written in its most standard form.

Standard Minor Blues Form

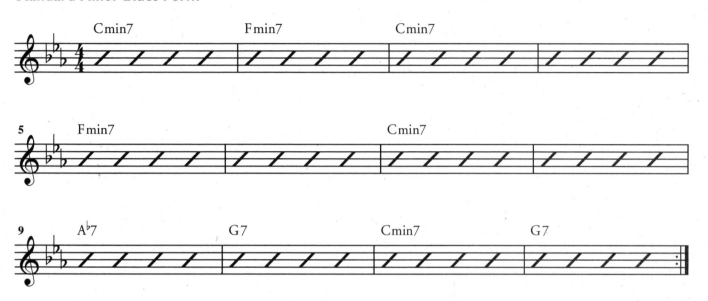

Following is a variation that uses a V chord followed by a iv chord in the last four bars.

Minor Blues Variation

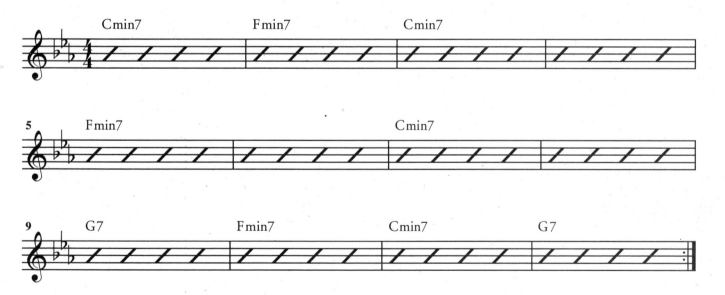

Although jazz musicians made substantial changes to the harmony and groove of the 12-bar blues, they always incorporated blue notes, blues-like phrasings, and blues riffs. The tune on the next page is a jazz-blues that features a walking bass line, swing feel, jazz-oriented chords, and melody.

"NY Subway Blues" is a 12-bar swinging jazz-blues in E♭ Minor. As you read the melody, pay close attention to the key signature and remember that it includes B♭, E♭, A♭, D♭, G♭, and C♭. Try playing the bebop-style melody twice and then take a solo as you play along with the recording. Since this song is written in a lead sheet style, much of it is left for you to interpret and improvise, including the left-hand chord voicings. Try *comping* (accompanying) using the sample voicings below to get started. When using these voicings, you will need to play the melody an octave higher so they don't collide. When you take a solo, try using the E♭ Blues scale, the E♭ Minor Pentatonic scale (all of the black keys on the piano), and arpeggios of the chord voicings with the right hand.

Sample Left-Hand Voicings for "NY Subway Blues"

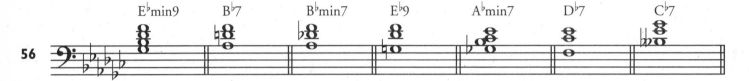

NY Subway Blues

Chapter 14: Funk, Soul, and Motown

Intro to Funk, Soul, and Motown

Starting in the 1960s, new genres of African-American popular music—styles rooted in the blues and influenced by gospel, as well as rhythm and blues—were emerging. These new genres, in turn, influenced the more traditional blues artists. The music of Ray Charles in the 1950s is often cited as the first example of what would come to be called "soul" music. By the 1960s, there was a plethora of soul artists recording on a number of record labels known for their influence on the musical style. Throughout the 1960s and 1970s, Stax Records, Motown Records, and the Muscle Shoals Sound Studio released hit after hit by musicians like Wilson Pickett, Aretha Franklin, Otis Redding, Booker T. & the MG's, Smokey Robinson, The Temptations, The Four Tops, The Supremes, The Jackson 5, Marvin Gaye, Stevie Wonder, and others.

At about the same time, James Brown—a talented soul singer from Augusta, Georgia—was developing a new style of soul music called "funk." By simplifying the chord progressions and emphasizing the rhythmic element in his songs, he developed a new sound based on an intensely danceable groove. His innovations influenced other musicians and a number of bands began playing funk in 1970s, including Parliament-Funkadelic, Earth, Wind & Fire, Kool & the Gang, Tower of Power, The Meters, and Sly & the Family Stone.

Just as the blues influenced soul and funk music, these new styles influenced blues artists to incorporate funkier grooves into their style. Modern blues musicians like B. B. King, Albert Collins, Buddy Guy, and Robert Cray have had commercial success using funky grooves in their songs.

Sixteenth Notes

Playing funk grooves usually means playing musical ideas based on sixteenth notes. Sixteenth notes divide the quarter note into four equal parts, which means there are 16 sixteenth notes to a whole note, or in one measure of $\frac{4}{4}$. Each group of sixteenth notes is beamed together with a double beam. Sixteenth notes are counted like this: "1-e-&-ah, 2-e-&-ah, 3-e-&-ah, 4-e-&-ah," etc.

Below are some possible sixteenth-note rhythms.

Count: 1   e   &   ah   1   e   &   1   &   ah   1   e   ah

Sixteenth-Note Practice Ideas

To achieve a truly funky feel, you will need to practice incorporating sixteenth-note riffs into your vocabulary. Try practicing some of the funky riffs below.

The Motown Sound

Motown Records, based in Detroit, Michigan, produced a string of memorable hits in the 1960s and 1970s. On many of these hits, they achieved the same "sound," or style, by using the same instruments and recording techniques. They also did this, in part, by hiring a group of musicians known as The Funk Brothers to provide instrumental backings on their recordings. The Funk Brothers featured bassist James Jamerson and three keyboardists (Earl Van Dyke, Johnny Griffith, and Joe Hunter), as well as a variety of drummers, guitarists, and percussionists.

"Soul City Blues" (next page) is a blues in E♭ that recalls the kind of syncopated sixteenth-note bass line that James Jamerson played on many Motown songs. In contrast, the right hand plays a simple, singable melody. To get an authentic Motown sound, play this one on a Fender Rhodes and find a friend to accompany you on tambourine.

Soul City Blues

The Stax Records Sound

In Memphis, Tennessee, Stax Records also released several important soul records in the 1960s and came to be known nationally as a powerhouse of soul music production. Like Motown, they developed their own "Stax sound" by using the same rhythm section on many of the recording sessions. This group included the multi-instrumentalist Booker T. Jones. His band, Booker T. & the MG's, included most of the Stax session musicians, and their bluesy, soulful sound is an excellent example of the kind of music Stax records produced.

"Orange Peppers" is a straightforward play-along in the style of Booker T. & the MG's. It's a 12-bar blues in F Minor, with a strong shuffle feel. The piece is written here as a lead sheet. Play the melody twice through with a B-3 organ sound, and then improvise a solo for a few choruses.

Track 74 *Orange Peppers*

James Brown and Other Funky Styles

While Stax and Motown pumped out their soul hits, James Brown (1933–2006) was inventing his own kind of soul music called "funk." This new music relied on aggressive interlocking sixteenth-note riffs played by the rhythm section and punctuated by a horn section. The vocals were also repetitive, percussive, and added to the polyrythmic feel. Brown changed the primary accented beat in his music from the backbeat (beats 2 and 4) to the downbeat (beat 1). He called this "playing on the one," and it allowed for the interlocking patterns to create intensity over a two-bar phrase before resolving with a strong accent on the downbeat. At first, he used the blues progression but later shifted to long vamp sections of a single chord sustained for entire verses and chorus, only to change on the bridge. The innovations of James Brown had great appeal and influenced a number of other musicians to play the funk style. Funk, like the blues, influenced many styles of music that came after it, including disco, jazz, Afrobeat, hip-hop, contemporary R&B, gospel, and jam bands.

Dominant 7♯9 Chords

Funk songwriters were inspired by the extensions used in jazz harmonies. In jazz, these chords are played in quick succession; but in funk, they are vamped on for several phrases, resulting in an intense harmonic build-up. The most popular of these funk chords is a dominant 7♯9. This chord's formula is: 1–3–5–♭7–♯9. Since its most recognizable feature is the ♯9, it is often just called a *sharp nine* (♯9) chord. Another way to look at a ♯9 chord is that it includes both the major and minor 3rd (the ♯9 is enharmonically equivalent to the ♭3). In this way, it's a perfect bluesy chord because it emphasizes the blue note found between the major and minor 3rds and provides the tonal ambiguity so essential to the blues sound. See below for the chord in root position.

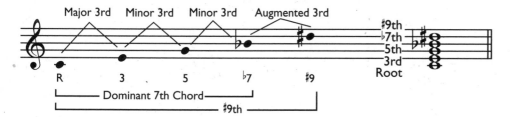

C Dominant 7♯9 Chord

The dominant 7♯9 chord is usually written enharmonically, like the following.

"How Mr. Brown Feels" is a funky 12-bar blues in the key of B. It features dominant 7♯9 chords and ensemble hits in the style of James Brown. Play the melody with your right hand and comp with your left. After two times through, solo over the chord changes without the hits.

How Mr. Brown Feels

PART 3: ADVANCED CONCEPTS

Parts 1 and 2 of this book covered music theory and the blues styles needed to be a proficient blues player. In Part 3, we will look at a variety of skills that will help you develop into an excellent, well-rounded blues musician.

Chief among these skills is the ability to play well with other musicians. Advanced concepts in improvisation and composition will also be addressed. Finally, we will look at important technical skills to practice.

Chapter 15: Playing in a Blues Band

While playing solo piano can be a rewarding experience because of its very personal challenges, there is something truly special about playing music with others. The sense of collective artistry and shared achievement brings musicians closer together on a personal level and allows the impact of the whole ensemble to exceed the combination of the individual contributions. In short, playing music with others is not only fun, but it can also be a soulful experience.

Most musicians will tell you there is one skill that is essential to good group playing. It can be summed up in a rule that goes like this, "listen more than you play." The idea is to be super-aware of what everyone else is playing so that you can craftily fit your part into the texture. If

you trust this heightened sense of listening, your instincts will answer any questions that come to mind and tell you what to play. If you are listening, you will know when to fill so that you don't jam up the space when others try to do the same. An open line of communication will help you determine when to solo. You will also be aware of the feel or groove of the song, select the appropriate volume, and lock in to a balanced performance.

When you play with different combinations of musicians, some specific concerns arise. The next few pages will address these issues so that you can be prepared to play with any type of blues ensemble.

Playing with Bass

Performing with a bass player is a liberating experience for a keyboard player. A good bassist holds down a solid groove, freeing up the keyboard player's left hand to do a number of different things. When a bass player is playing a specific, repetitive bass line, you can choose to double it with your left hand, or provide a complementary accompaniment. Try playing a barrelhouse left-hand pattern while the bassist plays a Chicago-style bass line. Use your ears to listen for clashing notes and adjust accordingly.

If the bass player is playing a walking line, try playing left-hand chords in a repetitive, rhythmic pattern. Remember, this is called "comping," which is short for accompanying. Jazz pianists are very good at leaving the root of the chord out to allow the bass player more room to create their line. Whatever you choose to do with your left hand, your right hand will be free to fill, solo, or play melodies independently.

Playing with Guitar

Much of what is true about playing with a bass applies to playing with guitar and other keyboard instruments. If done correctly, it can free you up to play interactively. The main concern when playing with other "chording" instruments is that you are in harmonic agreement; you need to be sure that you are playing the same chords. On a simple blues this shouldn't be much of a problem, but on songs with extensions or substitutions, you need to be aware of each other's chord voicings and listen for anything that clashes. Just like when you play with a bass player, you can choose to perform the same thing or develop complementary parts. Try holding down a bass part in your left hand while the guitar plays the chords. This will allow your right hand to do treble fills and chords. You could also try playing a left-hand bass line and right-hand chords in the middle register while the guitarist or other keyboard player solos. In both of these situations, you will be playing all of the parts in different registers, and will be out of each other's way.

Playing with Singers, Horns, and Harmonica

When you play with melodic instruments—even if you are accompanying your own voice—it's important to keep a few things in mind. When playing with vocalists, horns, or a harmonica (a.k.a. blues harp) player, your main role is usually to provide chordal accompaniment. You need to be sure to play all of the necessary harmonic and rhythmic information so they can listen to you and feel confident in their performance of the melody. You must also listen to them and not play fills or solos while they are trying to execute phrases of the melody or their own improvisations. Listen for them to take a breath or rest. If there is room, you can provide an improvised response to their call.

For singers, it helps to know their key of choice for a song. The human voice has a limited range, so singers generally have specific keys in mind for certain songs. Be sure to ask them about it before you start playing. If they are not sure, ask them to sing a few bars and try to find the key. Harmonicas also require attention to key. Harmonica players often bring a number of different "harps" with them, one for each key. So be sure to discuss the key, so they can select the appropriate harmonica from their collection.

Saxes and trumpets are *transposing* instruments, which means they sound in keys other than what they are written in. When you communicate with horn players about keys, be aware that the names of their keys are off from yours by a specific interval. For tenor sax and trumpet, the key of C is your key of B♭. For alto sax, the key of C is your key of E♭. To avoid confusion, refer to your key as being "concert," as in the "key of C concert," or "G concert." Then they will know that this means the non-transposed key and adjust accordingly.

Playing with Drums and a Full Band

There are very few things in music that are as exciting as playing with a good drummer. Solid drummers lay down a groove that is a joy to play over and interact with. When you play with a drummer, you are communicating rhythmic information to each other. All of the rhythms you play, and your general sense of the groove, must be "locked-in." That means they fit precisely together. That level of execution is not only achieved by being an accurate player, but also by both of you listening and aiming for rhythmic agreement.

Playing in a full blues band requires all of these skills at once. There are a few practical issues to keep in mind. One is your location on the bandstand. Many keyboardists want to be near the drummer because it helps them feel the groove. However, sitting next to the bass player offers better lines of communication. The bass player is providing both rhythmic and harmonic information. That makes them central to the band. It's a good idea to be on one side of the bassist, while the drummer is on the other. If you are singing, or if you are the bandleader, you may also choose to be out front, and allow the other musicians to form a semicircle behind you.

Wherever you choose to position yourself, it's important to keep the lines of communication and sight open to everyone in the band. There is a lot of information being communicated in many directions (see the chart below), so once again, listening is essential. Your ears will tell you when to play sparsely, in order to allow room for the others, and when to fill the space to drive the band. You may also want to "lay out," or stop playing at times, to allow for others to carry the groove. Keep the bandleader in your sight, and watch for cues for solos, endings, or stop-time. If you are the leader, you can provide these cues vocally, visually, or musically—but be sure they are clear.

Communication in a Blues Band

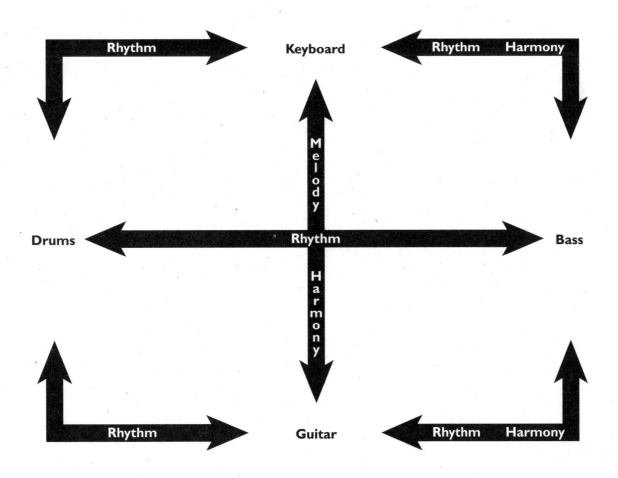

Chapter 16: Improvisation and Composition

Advanced Improvisation Ideas

By now, you likely have some skill at filling and soloing over the blues form. It's time for you to experiment with some advanced improvisation ideas. Since blues and jazz are closely related, most blues musicians are occasionally called upon to solo on something jazzy. This requires you to play some jazz-oriented eighth-note lines. These solo ideas, although rooted in the blues, can be quite different from standard riff- or lick-based blues ideas. Jazz players aim to create a flow of eighth notes in their solos. These jazzy lines touch on chord tones and extensions, and use chromatic notes to connect the pitches. Many jazz players think of their solo lines by associating scales with each of the chords in a song. The basic idea is that scales and chords are made from the same thing: groups of pitches. While scales are built horizontally, chords are built vertically, but they express the same harmony. Remember when we built the major triad from the major scale? Other chords can be seen as having been built from other scales. Figuring out what scales are associated with what chords is a matter of reversing that process.

Jazz players sometimes use blues scales to solo on a blues, but they also use a variety of other scales, some of which are outside the scope of this book. However, the most common choices for jazz-style soloing over dominant 7th chords in a blues are the *Mixolydian mode* and the *bebop scale*. The Mixolydian mode is similar to the major scale but with a ♭7 instead of a 7. Its formula is: R(1)–2–3–4–5–6–♭7. This allows the scale to fit perfectly over the dominant 7th chord built on the same tonic note.

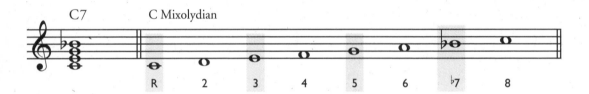

The bebop scale is similar to the Mixolydian mode, but it includes both the ♭7 and 7. The scale's formula is: R(1)–2–3–4–5–6–♭7–7. Again, the chord and scale are built on the same root.

Try to invent eighth-note ideas using these scales and chromatic notes to encircle or enclose chord tones. Think of the scale as a collection of notes you can use to generate improvisation ideas, not as something to be played verbatim. Playing the scale up and down over and over again wouldn't be very interesting to listen to. Skip around, and try some engaging combinations of notes. If you need more notes to complete your eighth-note phrase, add some chromatic notes to get you to your destination.

Unlike the blues scale, the Mixolydian mode and bebop scale are associated with specific chords, not the whole song. When you use these scales, you must adjust them for each of the 7th chords in the song; each chord gets its own scale. Check out the example below.

Building a Solo

The most artistic aspect of improvising is how you shape a solo. You can do this by changing the intensity of the solo over time. Think of how many choruses you wish to solo on, and begin to build the intensity accordingly. The overall shape of a good solo is like the plot curve of a good book or movie (see chart below). It begins rather mellow and adds tension to a point near the end, then resolves the tension to provide closure. A good blues solo tells a story that reflects on the lyrics or the melody of the song.

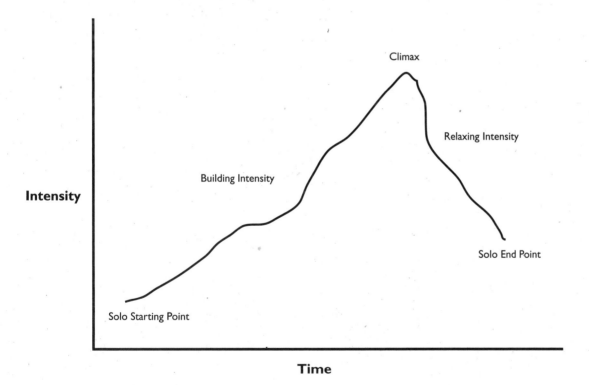

There are many ways to build intensity as you solo. Melodically, you can change the register and expand the chromaticism. Rhythmically, you can increase the rhythmic density or insert exciting, syncopated ideas. Harmonically, you can add superimposed chords or substitutions as you go along. You can also increase the volume or alter your tone as you solo. All of these ideas build tension and engage the listener. When you are ready to end the solo, relax the tension by reversing the process.

Composing Your Own Blues

Eventually, you may want to compose your own blues. Composing is a great outlet for your own creativity and self-expression. Composing and improvising are closely related. In fact, improvising is essentially composing in the moment—spontaneous composition. When you compose, you have plenty of time to consider your musical choices carefully. Often, songwriters talk of being inspired and letting the music flow out of them. While this type of writing does exist, composing also involves a number of choices to be made on a conscious level.

If you are not sure how to get started, think about all of the vocabulary you know and ask yourself, "What will the style or the groove be like? What will the harmony or form be like? Do I already have a melodic idea or blues riff in mind?" Perhaps you know the answers to some of these questions, and maybe you don't. Maybe you have a vague sense of the direction you want your song to take. This is your starting point. From there, you can improvise and experiment to find the complete answers to these questions. Engage the ear and the mind to compose, listen and edit. If you get stuck, reverse the process to edit, listen, and compose. As you work, keep in mind that if it sounds good to you, it's likely that it will sound good to others as well.

Below is some space for you to try writing a blues; use it to fully notate, or just sketch, some ideas.

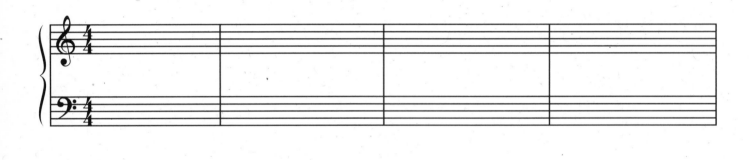

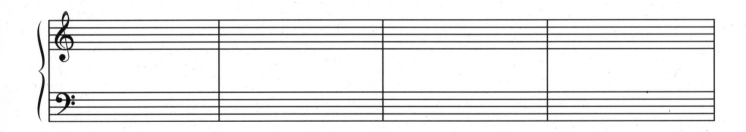

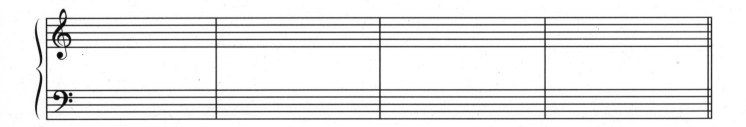

Chapter 17: Advanced Techniques

While it's easy to make a sound on a keyboard, mastering the instrument is quite difficult. Very few musicians become virtuosos. Those who do, can play almost anything composers imagine, no matter how difficult. This chapter explores some concepts that will help you on your journey to blues keyboard virtuosity.

Playing in Octaves

Whether it's classical piano concertos, jazz, salsa, or blues, there are a few common techniques that set the master keyboardists apart from the amateurs, or even the proficient professionals. One of these techniques is the ability to play melodies or solos in multiple octaves. This can be very useful in a blues band because it allows you to be heard more readily over the rest of the group. There are a variety of ways this can be done. Look at the simple melody below. Play it first with the right hand, then add the left an octave below. If you are like most keyboardists, your left hand is slightly weaker and less fluid than your right. Practice the left hand separately until it is as strong as the right. Then play them together again.

Now try playing the same idea, with the hands spread two octaves apart. It's important to visualize the line as being led by the weaker hand. If you do so, you won't attempt to exceed its ability and stumble. For ease, if there are grace notes, slides, or other ornaments, you can leave them out of the lower octave. Playing them only in the upper octave will give the illusion that you are playing them with both hands.

You can also play octave melodies with one hand, or the other, alone. Take the right hand and spread your reach so that the thumb (1) and the pinky (5) are positioned to span the interval of an octave. Now, use your arm to articulate the notes. Try adding another octave in the left hand. For a huge sound, try playing both hands in octaves. That's four octaves at once!

Rolling Octaves

Another way to play octaves is to *roll* them. That means to play them in quick succession rather than together. Try this first with your right hand, using triplets as notated below.

Now, try it using both hands in either direction.

You can even try it in four octaves using sixteenth notes.

Basic Block Chord Ideas

The same way you can "lock" your hands into playing octaves, you can lock them into playing melodies with entire chords. This is called playing *block chords*. There are a few different styles of block chords because several jazz pianists used them to develop their own personal styles. To get started, let's look at a basic version. Start with your right-hand 5th finger playing the melody. Double this with your left hand an octave lower. Now, fill in the chord notes with the rest of the right hand; the notes you choose can be notes that fit the chord, scale, upper extensions, or anything else that sounds good. In the example below, the first two phrases use parallel major 6th chords, each based on a note from the C Blues scale. The final phrase uses an arpeggiation of a D Minor chord, followed by more chromatically moving chords. Try experimenting with block chords to perform melodies, or to harmonize your solos.

Track 83 — Shoe Shop Blues

Fast Playing

Quickly executed runs and solos can add sparkle to any piece of music, but playing fast does not come easily. It requires good technique and lots of practice. The best way to execute fast lines fluidly is to use a *scratching* technique. This is when the fingers lightly articulate the keys while the arm moves fluidly in the direction of the line. The keys are depressed without full weight, resulting in a light "scratching" of the keys. They are pressed down just far enough to cause the hammer to touch the string, but no farther. This allows for maximum efficiency and fast playing. The faster you want to play, the more you will have to lighten your touch. It helps to find fingerings that make the lines you want to play flow easily. This will help you avoid the pitfall of awkward motions. Practicing scales with the motion of the thumb crossing under, and fingers crossing over, will help, as it will lead to long-term muscle memory. This will allow you to play lines without always thinking, "thumb under now." Your fingers will just know to do it. Finally, practice with a metronome to be sure you are not rushing or dragging at the tempo. Be conscious of whether you are playing sixteenth notes, triplets, or even sixteenth-note triplets when you improvise. Try playing the example below.

Advanced Concepts

There are a few overarching concepts that are important to focus on as you develop excellent technique. These will help you to play anything fluidly and musically.

Arm Weight

While it's the fingers that touch the keys, it's really the arm that provides the tone quality on weighted-key keyboard instruments. Playing with good arm weight relieves pressure on the wrists and provides a rich, rounded tone on the piano and electric pianos. Try playing a scale with just the fingers, and then with the arm fully engaged. Think of the sound coming from the shoulder and elbow, and you will hear the difference.

Gesture

Associated with arm weight is *gesture*. This is sometimes called *keyboard choreography*. Phrases at the keyboard have direction and motion. It's important to engage the arm in the arc of the phrase. For example, when you play a scale, lead naturally with the elbow. When you play a repeated arpeggio, the elbow and wrist make a natural circular motion. It is important to do these naturally and relaxed, so that they improve the tone and phrasing. If they are forced, they can have the opposite effect.

Hand Independence

When the two hands need to make different gestures at the same time, hand independence is required. It's a bit like patting your head and rubbing your tummy at the same time. Hand independence is essential for blues styles like boogie woogie and barrelhouse. With these styles, be sure to practice the hands separately and then together slowly. Memorize the independent gestures with your muscles and slowly work them up to speed.

Finger Strength

Finally, developing finger strength is also important. It is essential, however, that you don't rely on finger strength alone. It's no substitute for good arm weight and gesture. The first step to good finger technique is to be sure that your hand is achieving the rounded position (see page 9). Look for fingers, especially the pinkies, that are sticking out straight when you play a piece of music. This happens often in scale-based runs. If you find that this is the case, slow the passage down and consciously relax the offending fingers. Do this slowly many times slowly until the relaxed, rounded hand technique feels natural.

A great exercise for developing finger strength and independence is to press all five fingers down on the keyboard. Use the five white keys ascending from middle C (right-hand thumb on C, 2 on D, 3 on E, and so on). Then, play four quarter notes with each of the fingers while the other notes are still held down by all of the other fingers. This is particularly challenging to do with the 4th finger because of the anatomy of the hand. Try this exercise with both hands and, in time, you will notice an improvement in finger strength.

Conclusion

The end of this book is not the end of your pursuit of blues keyboard mastery. While this book offers the essential tools to any aspiring blues keyboardist, it probably raises a few questions as well. As a wise music teacher once said, "The answers are in the recordings; listen and learn." To get you started with this, the following pages feature lists for suggested listening, broken down by genre.

As you continue to develop as a musician, remember to experiment, innovate, play as much as you can, and have fun.

Suggested Listening

Collections

Atlantic Blues, Various Artists (Atlantic Records) 4-Disc Box Set

Blues Essentials, Various Artists (Capital Records)

Blues Masters, Vol. 1–15, Various Artists (Rhino Records)

Essential Blues Piano, Various Artists (House of Blues)

Piano Blues Soundtrack, Various Artists (Columbia Records)

Delta Blues

Robert Johnson: The Complete Recordings, Robert Johnson (Columbia Records)

The Original Delta Blues, Son House (Sony Records)

Barrelhouse Blues

New Orleans Barrelhouse Boogie, Champion Jack Dupree (Columbia Records)

New Orleans Blues

Crawfish Fiesta, Professor Longhair (Alligator Records)

Rum and Coke, Professor Longhair (Rhino/WEA)

Dr. John Plays Mac Rebbenack, Dr. John (Clean Cuts)

Chicago Blues

The Definitive Collection, Muddy Waters (Geffen Records)

The Chess 50th Anniversary Collection: Muddy Waters, Muddy Waters (Chess/MCA Records)

Blues by Roosevelt Sykes, Roosevelt Sykes (Smithsonian Folkways)

The Blues Never Die, Otis Spann (Prestige Records)

Boogie Woogie and Jump Blues

Boogie Woogie, Stride and Piano Blues, Various Artists (EMI Records)

King of Boogie Woogie, Albert Ammons (Acrobat)

The Blues Piano Artistry of Meade "Lux" Lewis, Meade "Lux" Lewis (Riverside/OJC)

Pete's Blues, Pete Johnson (Savoy Jazz)

Ragtime and Stride

Scott Joplin: King of the Ragtime Writers, From Classic Piano Rolls (Biograph Records)

The Original James P. Johnson 1942–1945, James P. Johnson (Smithsonian Folkways)

Chocolate to the Bone, Barbeque Bob (Yazoo)

Organ Blues

Hoochie Coochie Man/Got My Mojo Workin', Jimmy Smith (Verve Records)

Back at the Chicken Shack, Jimmy Smith (Blue Note Records)

Rock and Roll/Rhythm and Blues

20th Century Masters: Jerry Lee Lewis, Jerry Lee Lewis (Mercury Nashville)

Greatest Hits, Fats Domino (Capitol Records)

The Very Best of Little Richard, Little Richard (Specialty)

Birth of Soul, Ray Charles (Atlantic Records) 3-CD Set

Jazz Blues

Everyday I Have the Blues, Count Basie and his Orchestra with Joe Williams (EMI)

Bird's Best Bop on Verve, Charlie Parker (Verve)

Funk, Soul, and Motown

James Brown 20 All Time Greatest Hits!, James Brown (Polydor/UMGD)

Motown Classics Gold, Various Artists (Motown)

Stax 50th Anniversary Celebration, Various Artists (Stax Records)

The Muscle Shoals Sound, Various Artists (Rhino/WEA)

Modern Blues

Live and Well, B. B. King (MCA Records)

Live at the Cook County Jail, B. B. King (MCA Records)

The Very Best of Albert King, Albert King (Stax Records)

The Definitive Buddy Guy, Buddy Guy (Shout Factory)

Some Rainy Morning, Robert Cray (UMVD Special Markets)

Johnny B Bad, Johnnie Johnson (Nonesuch)